Born and Raised in Waikiki

Born and Raised in Waikiki

Betty Dyer Sorensen

A Limu Press Book
2511 East Cliff Drive
Santa Cruz, CA 95062

Born and Raised in Waikiki
ISBN 0-9645631-7-7
Copyright © by Betty Dyer Sorensen, 1995
All rights reserved

To order:
Limu Press 209-733-5590
Booklines Hawaii 808-676-0116

Second Printing

Dedication

This book is dedicated to all the people who have loved Waikiki in the past and who love it today, despite all the hotels and the clutter. The ocean, the palm trees and the beautiful mornings will always be there.

Thanks

Mary Dyer Sorensen Reath for editorial advice and devotion. Rebecca Laughlin for hours and hours on the design of the book. Andy Cummings for permission to use the words to "Waikiki." Tim Ryan, Gamma Liaison, for the cover photo. David Pietsch for the early Waikiki deeds. Holly Ketron, Monica Mayper and Fran Reath for copy editing and proof reading. Lu Hummel, Catherine Maldonado, Pauline Friedman, and Emi Sasaki for their in-put. Jim Sorensen for his belief in me. Collectors Reprints Inc. of New York City.

Table of Contents

CHAPTER 1
Waikiki, 1922 1

CHAPTER 2
My Dad 7

CHAPTER 3
Mabel Corrine DeJarlais 14

CHAPTER 4
Growing Up 20

CHAPTER 5
Living in Waikiki 28

CHAPTER 6
The Dole Derby 41

CHAPTER 7
My First Trip to the Mainland 44

CHAPTER 8
Magical Waikiki 49

CHAPTER 9
Getting Older 60

CHAPTER 10
Mokuleia Beach 68

CHAPTER 11
Dyer's Gift Shop 77

CHAPTER 12
Opportunity Knocks 82

CHAPTER 13
To the Orient 88

CHAPTER 14
Jack and Mabel 101

CHAPTER 15
My Faith **113**
CHAPTER 16
Around the World **119**
CHAPTER 17
On My Own At Last **131**
CHAPTER 18
December 7, 1941 .... **139**
CHAPTER 19
Graduation and the War Effort **148**
CHAPTER 20
Waikiki Wartime Dating **157**
CHAPTER 21
Waikiki Investors **166**
CHAPTER 22
World War II Ends **171**
CHAPTER 23
I'm Not Going To Be An Old Maid After All **176**
CHAPTER 24
Homesick **186**
CHAPTER 25
The Family Grows **191**
CHAPTER 26
Brain Surgery **205**
CHAPTER 27
Jim Sorensen **210**
CHAPTER 28
Haina Ia Mai Kapuana (This is the End of My Story) .. **221**

"Waikiki"

*"Waikiki, at night when the shadows are falling,
I hear your rolling surf calling,
Calling and calling to me.*

*Waikiki, 'tis for you that my heart is yearning,
My thoughts are always returning,
Out there to you, across the sea."*

Words and music by Andy Cummings

CHAPTER 1

Waikiki, 1922

"... just one block from Waikiki Beach."

Mother always told me that when she went into labor, my father refused to drive her to the hospital right away.

He had to shave!

From that, I guess I was destined to always be waiting for some man to do what he had to do.

It was 1922, and Mother and Dad and my six-year-old brother, Jack, were living in the house at 290 Beach Walk in Waikiki, just one block from Waikiki Beach.

Waikiki was a small neighborhood then, with little cottages, inexpensive apartments and a few nice houses. People liked to live there because it was so close to the ocean and to transportation. The streetcars went down Kalakaua Avenue, Waikiki's main thoroughfare, all the way from Diamond Head to the business section of downtown Honolulu, three miles away. The few tourists who visited either stayed with friends for at least a month or they rented a cottage. The Moana Hotel was on the beach, with their cottages and tennis courts across the street; the Royal Hawaiian Hotel was on the drawing board.

Born and Raised in Waikiki

Mother and Dad bought the 7055-square-foot lot for $1500 in 1918 from a spinster named Alice Knapp who had bought it for $850 in 1915.

They had the house built to their design and it was home to me until I married in 1946. Later on, in the Fifties, the property became very valuable and Mother and Dad leased it to a developer for a hotel site, but that is getting too far ahead of the story.

Dad came to Hawaii around 1910 with his partner, Mr. Dave Endleman. They had traveled to the West Coast from Ohio to look around for business opportunities. They observed the Hollywood movie business and decided it was not for them, and continued west with an eye on the Orient. As Dad told me, "We had made a lot of money conducting close-out sales all over the Midwest and the East, and we were looking for new opportunities."

Endleman didn't care for Hawaii's climate, but my father fell in love with the climate and *all* of it. Dad lived out the rest of his life in Honolulu and did not go back to his hometown until twenty-three years after he'd arrived.

My mother was born on a ranch in northern California, moved to San Francisco as a young woman, and after surviving the San Francisco earthquake of 1906, decided to try life in Hawaii.

When Dad and Mom were married, they originally planned their wedding on mother's birthday, October 12, 1915, but she heard it was bad luck to be married on one's birthday. She was thirty-one years old and not looking for bad luck, so they postponed the wedding until October 20.

They had a morning wedding at St. Augustine's Chapel in Waikiki with Father Valentine officiating, followed by a

Waikiki, 1922

champagne breakfast. My dad was thirty-seven. Both were born and raised Catholic, and this was their first marriage. Mother's engagement announcement was in the newspaper, and I was always very proud of it because she looked beautiful, dignified, and sophisticated. Lucky for them the wedding had been delayed a week because otherwise they might not have met the couple who were to be their best friends for the rest of their lives.

After the wedding breakfast and reception, they were driven over the Pali and around to Hauulu to a resort called Cooper's Ranch. It was far off the road and sort of nestled next to the Koolau mountains, cool and quiet, and ideal for a honeymoon.

For years afterward, we used to stop there for lunch when we drove tourists around the island. We kids liked to go there because they had chickens, and we could be excused from the boring grown-up talk and allowed to wander around the grounds chasing the chickens.

Another honeymooning couple were Clara and Hugo Ludders. Clara was Irish Catholic from San Francisco and Hugo was German-born and strict. She had a generous heart, and a hearty laugh, and they all played excellent bridge. From then on, they were a foursome.

Clara had a little car, and one day she was driving her daughter, Sally, past the Royal Mausoleum on Nuuanu Street.

"This is where they bury the kings and queens."

And little Sally piped up, "Where do they bury the *jacks*?"

Clara was a marvelous cook. She and my mother competed for the lightest and the highest cake. My mother won that contest, but Clara won for the lightest dinner rolls. They also used to get out the tape measure to see which one had the skinniest legs. They would laugh and laugh at this contest.

For many years we traded back and forth at holidays. We'd get very dressed up when we went to the Ludders' house. Dad would wear his white dinner jacket and black tie. and Mom would wear a long dinner gown and her crystal beads and earrings. It was during the depression years, but we were dressing to the nines anyway.

Being in Honolulu meant we didn't have relatives to speak of, and so we spent holidays with friends. Dad usually took us to the Royal Hawaiian Hotel for Easter Sunday lunch. Sometimes another family went with us, and we all got very dressed up and paraded ourselves proudly through the magnificent lobby of the Royal. Before we walked into the dining room, we stopped to admire the enormous arrangement of hibiscus flowers stuck on coconut-palm-frond spines so that each hibiscus could be individually admired.

Some things never change, and by the time I actually stayed at the Royal Hawaiian Hotel years later in 1982, the hibiscus (orchids nowadays) display was still a daily feature of the lobby—redone every day for over sixty years.

We kids drove our dads wild because we filled up on rolls and water. Dad would sit there glowering as we helped ourselves to another roll and more ice water every time the waiter came by. We were also crazy about the ice-cold butter pats. They tasted so divine, and we weren't sure how the next course would taste. The dads were paying $4 each for this special dinner. Of course, there was soft

Waikiki, 1922

Hawaiian music or sometimes classical music by a string quartet.

We all made a big show of loosening our belts at least one notch. By this time my father was more than ready to say *Check, please,* and we kids were dying to be excused so we could walk out and look at the ocean, the surfers, and the people lying on the beach. That part hasn't changed, only the $4 is probably $40 today!

Clara and Mother had both lived in San Francisco during the 1906 earthquake and fire. They spent hours recalling the horrors and trading stories and even laughing at some of their experiences. Clara could laugh even in the face of despair, as we found out many years later after World War II began. She remained my mother's most faithful friend all of Mother's life.

The following letter is one Mother wrote to us in 1952, looking back at her experiences in San Francisco the day of the 1906 earthquake. I quote from the letter:

> *My dear ones: Just 46 years ago today, April 18, your Mother-to-be was walking the torn-up streets of San Francisco after a most terrific earthquake. All my possessions consisted of a suitcase of wearing apparel. The rest I had to leave behind. I left my home at 108 McAllister Street with a suitcase and a small trunk, to which I had a kitchen apron attached, and I dragged it along the street in that fashion. The first night I stayed in Calvary Cemetery, right at the edge of it and slept on the cement sidewalk. The result was a bad case of pleurisy. The next morning I walked to Van Ness Avenue and thence to the beach and followed the beach until I came to the Ferry Building. There I caught a boat*

Born and Raised in Waikiki

across the bay to Oakland.

I lived on McAllister Street in a rooming house my father had invested in after he sold out our ranch. The lamp posts, car tracks, etc., were badly twisted and the streets were filled with debris. There were places where the earth's crust was cracked and laid open, places 10 feet across or more in length and several feet across. By the time we reached Oakland my face was black as could be. I called Mr. Wetmore, head of the concern where I worked, The Cresta Blanca Wine Company, and the Wetmore's invited us to their lovely home where I got something to eat, a much needed bath and went to bed somewhere in the mid-afternoon. I slept through until early the next morning when I boarded the train for Willows, our old home town. There my sister met me and most of the people of this little town were at the depot to see who might be coming home. After a stay with my sister, Laura, she and I took the train for Carson City where our brother Oliver was running a hotel my father had bought.

Across the street from that rooming house on McAllister was the Hall of Records, a large cement building with a round dome. It took a long time to build but went down in seconds.

Your Mother

CHAPTER 2

My Dad

"We all held our breath for the moment of utter nakedness."

Dad was forty-four when I arrived to shatter his calm. Of course he was glad to see me but at his age, and with six-year-old Jack already throwing blocks all over the house, he was beginning to want a little peace and quiet. Mother told me he did not come home for dinner for the first three years of my life. He ate at the Blaisdell Hotel.

Normally, he closed his store, Dyer's Gift Shop, every day Monday through Saturday at 5:00 and walked down Fort Street to the corner of King Street right by Benson Smith's Drug Store, and there he would hop onto the streetcar that went to Waikiki. The streetcar went toward Waikiki on King Street and then it made the sweeping turn onto Kalakaua Avenue. One could see water buffalo in the taro field there. The center divider was already planted with coconut trees, and in the winter the poinsettias were wildly blooming in huge bushes.

Dad stepped off the streetcar right in front of our house on the corner of Kalakaua Avenue and Beach Walk. I think I can still see him swing his long legs off the step, wearing a white pongee suit. The streetcars were open on both sides, and men would ride on the outside steps. Kids couldn't, of course. Dad loved to ride there in the breeze.

When our dog, Kam (*Kamehameha*), heard my dad's approaching footsteps, he would run and hide or run and push open the back screen door and get out of the house as fast as he could. Dad and Kam avoided each other for their mutual peace of mind. Much later they became best friends. Kam won him over, but Dad still hated cats to the end of his life and would turn the hose on them whenever he could.

He was six feet tall and always slender. When I was born, he had been in business for about twelve years. His store was on the corner of Fort Street and Chaplain Lane, so named I suppose because the cathedral, Our Lady of Peace, was and still is just across the street on the Diamond Head side of Fort Street. He had been introduced to Mabel DeJarlais from San Francisco by a friend and later on he had observed her going into the cathedral and so he supposed she was also Catholic. Since he was Catholic, he became even more interested.

For the sake of history, I should tell you that the famous priest to the lepers of Molokai, Father Damien de Veuster, was ordained at Our Lady of Peace in May of 1864. Father Damian left his home in Belgium as a missionary for the Sacred Hearts, an order of priests and nuns and brothers. He arrived in Honolulu on the Feast Day of St. Joseph, March 19, 1864. His was one of the first ordinations in that cathedral. In 1873, he went to Molokai and ministered there until he died as a leper in 1889. Statues of him and King Kamehameha represent Hawaii in the Capitol Rotunda in Washington, D.C.

My Dad

And so my Dad operated his store for thirty-five years on that corner. He boasted that he never had a sale in all those years. Once in a while he would come home chuckling about something that had happened that day in the store.

The story I remember most was about a Honolulu matron who would go into the store at least once a week and try on a thirty-six inch strand of amber beads and take up Dad's time asking questions about the price and the quality and blah blah blah. (If anyone ever questioned the authenticity of amber, Dad would toss the beads into the air and let them fall to the floor; amber, a fossil resin, would not break as glass would.) After several *months* of this she strode into the store one day and grandly announced to my dad that she had decided to purchase the beads!

He, at that point, sensed revenge, and so he refused to sell them to her. She snatched the beads, pulled them to her bosom and demanded that he sell them to her. With his eyes blazing, he grabbed the beads back. This tug-of-war went on and on and my dad never let up. Finally, the woman gave up and stomped out in disgust.

When he came home that evening and told us the story, he was laughing so hard that he could hardly talk. He felt vindicated for all the pain and indignity that that woman had inflicted on him. We all wished we had been there to witness it! We could see his blue eyes flashing with red sparks. He loved to tell that story.

My father was a real go-getter and a hero to his sisters in Ohio. I can imagine they talked about him every day and twice on Sundays. He was very handsome as you can tell from his pictures. His blue eyes looked one squarely in the eye, and he twinkled when he grinned. His hair started out being reddish, and he could get a mean sunburn, as his skin was very white. His father served for three years in the Army of the Cumberland during the Civil War: a member of company C of the 21st Illinois Reg. When his father was mustered out at the end of the war, he married an Irish Catholic girl with a fierce temper. She was six feet tall and so she and I could have looked each other in the eye.

My father's five sisters adored the ground he walked on. He was successful, and we respect success very much in the Dyer family. Mother got along well with her five sisters-in-law. That was not too hard to do, since she lived in Honolulu and they all lived in Ohio.

My aunts were excellent cooks. There was Kate, the oldest and unmarried. She remained unmarried in order to look after her father when my grandmother died. (Possibly the real reason was that she had terrible halitosis.) There was Sadie (Sarah), who married and had one daughter who in turn had one son, my cousin Lewis Johnston. The third sister was Anne, who married a medical doctor, Henry Washburn, and had one daughter, my cousin Mary. Anne's husband died in the flu epidemic after World War I. The fourth sister was Nellie, who entered the convent of the Seaton Sisters of Charity and never looked back. Her father made her promise she would call him if she needed help, but she never called.

Aunt Nell taught first graders for fifty years. In her religious life she was called Sister Norberta, but to us she was Aunt Nellie. She was barely five feet tall and had huge blue eyes that devoured me with their kindness. I always wanted to hug her but it was hard to get a good grip on her

My Dad

when she was wearing her bonnet and her habit with its huge starched bib.

I think she loved her habit. She wore nun's shoes (black lace-ups with a one-inch heel) and a very long rosary around her waist and she walked with vigor and swished her skirts and rattled her beads as she walked. Because of the white bonnet she wore as part of her habit, she had to turn her head from side to side in order to see the person speaking to her unless, of course, you were sitting directly in front of her.

Aunt Nell always used to send me religious articles for Christmas and birthdays. It was always "Here's Aunt Nell's present. You *know* what's in there." Rosaries, prayer cards, and little plastic statues of the Blessed Virgin Mary or St. Joseph. I still have some somewhere. I was afraid to throw them away in case it was a sin.

The youngest, my dad's favorite, was christened Loretta, but was always called Aunt Lot. She married and immediately annulled her marriage and never tried it again. The story was that the fellow she married wanted to live with Aunt Lot and his mother at the same time. She would have none of it, and that was the end of her married life. She was a horrible snob. In fact, I think all the Dyers are a little snobby at times.

The two times I visited Springfield, Ohio, pronounced *Oh'hi'ya*, they stuffed me with all the fried chicken, mashed potatoes, and string beans I could eat. I remember loosening my belt so I could have another helping. They enjoyed every mouthful I ate. I can remember them all looking at me and waiting to see if I had the Dyer appetite and appreciation for fried chicken. We would all have to watch and admire while Aunt Sadie cut into her famous black walnut cake.

"It's so high, it's so tender and moist, etc, etc."

By the time I met them all for the first time in 1933, Aunt Sadie's daughter, Louise, and her son Lewis, were living in the other side of the two-family house. Louise's husband had also died in the flu epidemic. Some of these living arrangements might have been due to the depression. They lived comfortably but without ostentation.

One year, after I was old enough to take note of what my parents were talking about at the dinner table, I heard my mother say to my father, "Why don't you buy Louise a new car?" Mother was generous in that way, and so my father did send Louise money for a new car.

In 1933, my Dad was making his first trip back to Ohio since he left home at age fourteen. Since it was so special an occasion my Aunt Nell got permission from the Mother Superior to come home for a visit.

Aunt Lot gave me a facial, plucked my eyebrows, and put nail polish on my nails. My father had a livid fit. Remember, I was only eleven. He made me scrape off all the red polish, which I did on the train to Chicago after we left Springfield. We had stayed in Ohio exactly one week. I had walked around town barefoot, showing off my Hawaiian traditions, doing the hula for anyone who asked me.

In Chicago, we took in the World's Fair Century of Progress. We saw the flea circus, with little fleas dressed up and hopping in circles. We also saw Sally Rand do her fan dance.

Dad and I sat in the balcony of the darkened theater anticipating something sensational. My hands were damp

My Dad

and my nerves expectant. The audience was rapt and restless, and when Sally came out with her two enormous ostrich feather fans and started to flutter them back and forth in front of her and in back of her in graceful time to the slow music, we all held our breath for the final *moment of utter nakedness*. When the music crescendoed and the drums rolled and our hearts began to pound it was almost unbearable. In a crashing burst of cymbals she dropped the fans and the lights went *off* and everyone clapped and whistled, and then we looked around and said, "That's *IT*? Is that *ALL* there is?"

We got some sense of satisfaction when we got back to Honolulu and could tell everyone we had seen Sally Rand do her fan dance. Big deal. Being eleven years old, I preferred the fleas.

We stayed at the Palmer House in Chicago, and I took delight in chewing my gum into a tight ball and then dropping it out the window onto the walkers way down below. We later traveled by train to Los Angeles and stayed at the Biltmore Hotel. (Years later I would find myself on the stage of the Biltmore Hotel singing Hawaiian songs.) We rode the red car to Long Beach where we took the steamship *Mariposa* back to Honolulu. We had been away from Honolulu a month. I probably had grown two inches.

CHAPTER 3

Mabel Corrine DeJarlais Dyer

"I'm not the governor but I'll pardon you!"

Mother arrived in Honolulu around 1913. She was twenty-nine years old and was looking for the man of her dreams. She took a civil service exam in typing and shorthand and passed with the highest grade. Every time we passed the beautiful Immigration building on Ala Moana across from Honolulu Iron Works, she would say to me, "That's where I worked."

Mother liked to talk about growing up on the ranch in Willows, in northern California. Her father, Francis Xavier De Jarlais, had been born in Trois-Rivieres in Quebec, Canada, as had her mother, Marie Picotte. They were French Canadians and were offered a section of land in California if they would homestead it, and so, sometime around 1870, they got to California and settled in the Sacramento Valley in a little town called Willows. All four of their children were born in Willows: Oliver, Wilfred, Laura, and Mabel, my mother.

Once Marie traveled on a sailing ship that left from Monterey, California, and had to go around the Horn in order to visit her family in Trois-Rivieres. She is the pioneer

Mabel Corrine DeJarlais Dyer

woman of our family. She died in Willows when my mother was only three years old.

Mom said her two brothers, Oliver and Wilfred, used to give grain to the chickens after it had been soaked in whiskey and then hold their sides laughing at the staggering chickens.

Mother always said her father fed all the widows and orphans in the town. She was proud of his generosity. He could also speak Spanish besides English and his native French, play the fiddle, and call the square dances. He wore a little black cap, and if one of the children got too loud at the table he would throw his cap at them.

Mother made her high school graduation dress all by hand. It was a lovely full-length creation of voile and lace with leg-o-mutton sleeves and a high collar. She was beautiful, with her dark hair done up in Gibson Girl style and her dark eyes shining. There were only three graduates in Willows that year, 1904.

Mother knew how to swim, and for many years enjoyed a dip to cool off. I have pictures of her taken on Waikiki Beach, and she looked very fetching in her long black stockings and black wool bathing suit with a large Japanese umbrella shading her face.

She made excellent sukiyaki, and we often took that to a club we belonged to in Waikiki, the Uluniu Club, which was next to the old Outrigger Canoe Club. Because my dad would not eat sukiyaki, he usually did not join us there. He wanted *everything plain* which translated to *no gravy, no sauce*. We would meet other families there and have a swim. We kids stayed in the water until our skin looked like white, wrinkled chicken skin.

Born and Raised in Waikiki

There was a girl who hung out in the ladies' locker room at the club who used to terrorize me by pulling my hair. I wish now I had stood my ground and bopped her one, but at the time I felt too intimidated. I finally asked my brother to go in and scare her. He did, and she left me alone after that. I really loved my big brother for that. He also used to swat the huge, ugly-looking spiders for me when they were up in the corners of the shower.

Mother was a gorgeous cook. She went to the cooking school at the Hawaiian Electric Company in the Thirties, and learned to present her dishes so that they looked just too good to eat. But we dug in, and soon I would say, "I'm full" and then Ma would repeat her ditty, "*I am so full I cannot pull another blade of grass. Baa, baa,*" and then laugh at the offender.

Jack got the same.

When we were growing up, Mom used a lace tablecloth from China on the dinner table just so it would be too uncomfortable for Jack to put his elbows on the table. It worked!

Mother called dinner the diversion of the evening, and she craved conversation when the meal was finished. My father came to the table to have dinner, and conversation was secondary. As soon as he was finished he wanted to leave the table. No conversation, unless we had visitors from the mainland, and then he became a brilliant raconteur.

Jack was a normal slob as a teenager, and since his room was in between the kitchen and the back hall, it was a room we used as a short cut. Both doors were usually open, and Pop would have a fit if Jack's room was littered with dirty clothes.

One day Mom taught Jack the lesson you never forget.

She literally swept all the clothes lying on the floor out the back door, and there they lay in the driveway. She hadn't planned on Dad getting home before Jack.

Holy cow! What a hullabaloo!

Dad got home first, slammed on the brakes, and blared the horn over and over and Mother ran out and reddened and tried to explain.

I, like the dog, ran and hid until the fireworks were over. Jack had to hear this story repeated several years running. In a way, the joke was on Mother.

Jack knew how to jolly her. She could get angry about something and chase me around the house with a stick, and I'd be begging, "Please don't hit me."

She'd chase Jack around with the same stick, and pretty soon I could hear them laughing. Like I said, he knew how to jolly her. I didn't.

Mom had worked for a judge in San Francisco, Judge Guggenheim, who had some pet peeves, and they became hers. One was saying *Pardon me*. The punch line was,

"I'm not the governor but I'll pardon you."

Another was to say *quite a few* instead of *quite a number*.

As Mom said, "There is no such thing as quite a few. Quite a *number* went to the beach but *only* a *few* went swimming."

She loved to cook. Cakes were her specialty, always beaten up by hand with a large wooden spoon in a large mixing bowl. The cube of butter went into the bowl before we left for church so it would be soft enough to beat with the sugar when we got home. She made her famous gold cake and a mile-high angel food cake. A dozen egg yolks in the first and the dozen egg whites in the second.

Later on she got one of the first electric mixers sold in Honolulu, but she never stopped stirring up her angel food cake by using a large heavy hotel-weight platter, large enough for a turkey, and slowly aerating the whites by using a wire whisk over and over the full length of the platter. It was a treat to watch the eggs begin to turn white, and the sugar to thicken up the whites and flour being sifted gradually over the whole batter until it was finally all mixed and ready for the baking.

I remember asking her before I was married how I would have the strength to eat after cooking a meal, and her dry reply, "Don't worry; you'll be hungry."

And she was right, of course.

If we wasted food, she would chant,

"Do not throw upon the floor the crumbs you cannot eat, for many a little hungry one would think it quite a treat."

"Pretty is as pretty does" was another harp.

And if you dared to say *I can't* about anything you were expected to do, you got, "Mr. *I can't* never did anything. Mr. *I'll try* is the one."

And if we weakly said we forgot she would shame us with, "Remember the man who forgot and all the lives were lost because one man forgot." She'd add, "He was the switchman on the railroad" as if we needed to be reminded.

Mother had a car of her very own and unlike Dad, she was a good driver. I remember driving down Ala Moana hanging over the front seat of the Buick sedan.

"Golly, Ma, you're going 25."

Mabel Corrine DeJarlais Dyer

She probably told me to, "Sit down and *shut up!*"

She was a cautious driver. She'd get disgusted at people who drove with their brakes and their horns instead of their heads. People used to honk their horns a whole lot back then. I remember driving over the Pali and my dad honking his horn before every curve. We went honk-honking from Honolulu to Kailua, hanging on to the cloth top of the car so it wouldn't blow off. At one time we drove a touring car with a cloth top. Believe you me, we all hung on to the top as we rounded the windy corner at the Pali summit. It was a common sight to see a car with its top blowing straight up.

My father, on the other hand, was a terrible driver. None of us wanted to ride with him. He was a horn-honker of the variety Mother disdained. He believed he was the world's finest man behind the wheel. He bragged about never having gotten a traffic ticket.

One day we were driving some tourists around the island and Dad was in his glory saying how he'd never had a ticket. As if on cue, the siren sounded and a cop pulled us over and handed him a speeding ticket. With a red face he had to go to court in Hauulu to pay a $10 fine. We retold that story often but not when *he* was around.

Francis Xavier deJarlais and his wife, Marie Picotte, Willows, California around 1870

John Michael Dyer before he went to Honolulu

Mabel deJarlais' engagement picture

Uncle Wilfred deJarlais, my mother's brother

*My dad's five sisters.
Left to right, Lottie, Kate, Nell, Sarah and Anne*

John Michael Dyer in downtown Honolulu in 1914

John and Mabel Dyer with Jack and Betty in 1922

Another view of the Moana Hotel and the private homes on the left. The trees that wave to me as I walk by. The top of the sea wall that people walk on even today

Nuuanu Pali, where the wind always blows

The Royal Hawaiian Hotel with Ulunui Club on the right

Duke Kahanamoku in front of The Outrigger Canoe Club

Our house on Beach Walk

My brother Jack and me by the "slop bucket"

My little piano

Jack and me

Betty and Jack leaving Parker Ranch with Mother, top right, and mother's nurse friend, top left

1160 Fort Street, Honolulu, Hawaii. Dyer's Gift Shop

Me, a friend, Marney Bellows and Eudora Levy

Aunt Laura Lear and me, 1926

Mrs. Macrafee's dancing class. Betty, front row right

Waikiki Kindergarten, 1926. Betty, top row right

Mabel Dyer on the beach at Waikiki

Little park on the corner of Kalakaua and Beach Walk

CHAPTER 4

Growing Up

"At times in the thirties, the lily pond was the scene of mass hysteria"

I loved going to Mrs. Macrafee's dancing class in Waikiki. She had henna-colored hair and wore purple shoes with high heels, not sensible laced-up shoes like my mother. I loved to dance and felt quite good at it. When I was four years old, we had a big recital at the Princess Theater in downtown Honolulu. It took place one evening before the movie started. I wore a white tutu which had gossamer wings outlined with tinsel. I felt outrageously pretty and like a star.

After the performance where I twirled around with all the other little girls, I took myself all by myself down into the front row of the theater and prepared to watch the movie.

My frantic mother found me, scolded me, and dragged me home and that ended a small taste of independence.

But I liked how it tasted!

Mother also arranged for me to take piano lessons. I loved Mrs. Gertrude Piutti, my sweet music teacher. Her house was on Royal Hawaiian Avenue just off Kalakaua. I could walk there from our house just two blocks away, and

Growing Up

I always loved to look at the handsome Gump's store on the corner of Lewers Road and Kalakaua Avenue.

It's a franchise fast food place now, but in the Thirties it was shopping paradise for the wealthy. It was an imposing two-story white stucco building with a Chinese blue tile roof and a moon gate as the entrance. Two huge blue-ceramic Foo dogs guarded the entrance on either side of the moon gate. When I got older, I ventured in to shop there, but I never got over my awe of the atmosphere. It was nothing like my dad's little store, but Gump's used to buy from us when they ran out of jade. I recall selling one of their salesladies an opera-length Imperial Jade necklace for our retail price of $250.00 knowing that Gump's would mark it up at least two times. We talked about their high prices as we ate dinner.

I loved music, and so despite my foibles I learned to play the piano. My dad wanted me to be a show girl, and he said I had to learn to sing and dance and to play the piano. He was a little dippy about all this, and I never really thought I'd be anything other than a housewife and mother. I thought his ambitions for me were ridiculous.

For my tenth birthday I received the biggest tricycle that was ever made. What I asked for was a two-wheel bicycle, but my dad thought I was too young and it would be too dangerous on the busy streets of Waikiki, and so he bought this huge tricycle for me. It was enormous but not as enormous as my disappointment. For the party we had cake and ice cream at our house, and afterwards, we all rode the two blocks over to the Royal Hawaiian Hotel grounds. My pals rode their skates on the hotel's sidewalks, and I followed on my tricycle, pedaling as fast as I could to keep up.

Born and Raised in Waikiki

The yard men saw us, but they didn't kick us out. In fact, we used the Royal Hawaiian Hotel as another one of our playgrounds. When we got older, we would boldly walk into the hotel's card room and play honeymoon bridge and order Coca-Colas and pretend we were rich tourists.

The most daring thing I did as a kid was to take a surreptitious ride on my brother's two-wheel bike. I had to have that ride! It was burning up inside me. When no one was looking, I hopped onto his bicycle and pedaled furiously around my block, down Beach Walk and back up on Saratoga Road.

It was exhilarating. No one ever knew.

I started at Punahou School in 1927. It had been founded in 1841 by the missionaries so that they wouldn't have to send their little ones to boarding school all the way from Hawaii to New England. The sons and daughters of the *alii* (Hawaiian chiefs) were also among some of the first students.

Punahou School welcomed all races living in Hawaii and encouraged as many as could afford it to get their education there. It was a wonderfully unprejudiced beginning. I started in first grade, and twelve years later, in 1939, I proudly graduated.

If one could see the campus, one might think it was a university. It has many beautiful buildings, large playing fields, several tennis courts, a huge swimming pool with bleachers for meets, ancient tropical trees, a stately avenue of palms, and a lava rock wall covered with night-blooming cereus. The most honored site on the campus is what is referred to as the lily pond. Tradition has it that the Hawaiians called the water in the pond

Growing Up

Ka Punahou, meaning, the new spring.

At times in the Thirties, the lily pond was the scene of mass hysteria. It would happen like this. A certain boy in the upper grades would be targeted by the other boys for whatever reason. This meant that that particular boy would be *pantsed* by the older boys and then with much shouting and laughter, the mob would haul that unfortunate and wildly protesting and struggling victim up to the lily pond and with a *one, a two and a three*, heave him into the air and with a huge splash, he would land in the lily pond.

It was terribly exciting, and we little lower school children were part of the throng because it always happened during recess. I remember watching and shivering with fear for the poor boy who was getting tossed. I wondered if my brother might be the next victim.

I recall the day some big tough kids from school arrived at our house in Waikiki looking for my brother, who was hiding. I don't know what they had against him but when my mother looked at them, she knew they were, up to something. One kid was nicknamed *Bull*, and Mom knew his reputation. She confronted them in their car in our driveway and chased them off.

My brother at that time was a scrawny, tall, pimple-faced tennis player. Through his own will and determination he studied the Charles Atlas manuals, the ones that said *"I was a ninety-pound weakling until I took up Charles Atlas."* Jack exercised and developed his body and his muscles, and he even went so far as to chew his milk. That was recommended by Atlas as a way to gain weight. He would take a sip of milk and then before he would swallow it he would chew it twenty times. Unbelievable, but it worked. He gained weight and developed a very nice physique, and eventually he taught himself to play excellent tennis. He studied all the photos in the tennis magazines and analyzed the players' positions and their grips and read all the accompanying articles.

He was totally dedicated to tennis, and eventually he and his doubles partner, Bo Ming Yee, won the doubles championship for all the Hawaiian Islands. Jack never allowed us to watch his matches. We went anyway and hid behind a tree and kept very quiet.

My brother and I liked to sing together. Our favorite was "The Prune Song."

> "No matter how young a prune may be
> it's always full of wrinkles,
> We may get them on our face,
> prunes get them every place."
> Prohibition bothers us
> but prunes don't sit and brood,
> For no matter how young a prune may be,
> it's always getting stewed."

Mother was the most fun on Maui or in Seattle or at Mokuleia, all places far removed from stress and responsibilities and my father. She let her hair down and would sing. Aunt Daisy Sabin lived at Puunene, Maui, and we would stay with her for a month or more. Aunt Daisy was not my real aunt, but we always called my mother's good friends *aunt*. She sure loved to sing too. Some of their favorites became mine—"Two Little Girls in Blue," "Let the Rest of the World Go By," "After the Ball," and more.

Growing Up

Mom also sang the songs she learned on the ranch. One song was,
> "Oh I went to the animal fair.
> All the birds and the beasts were there.
> The old raccoon ,by the light of the moon,
> Was combing his auburn hair.
> The monkey he got drunk
> And fell on the elephant's trunk.
> The elephant sneezed and fell on his knees
> And what became of the monk, the monk."

Another was unique.
> "Down in the hen house on my knees.
> Lord a bless a lamb and a glory hallelujah.
> I thought I heard a chicken sneeze.
> Lord a bless a lamb and a glory hallelujah.
> Only a rooster saying his prayers.
> Singing a hymn to the hens upstairs.
> Lord a bless a lamb and a glory hallelujah."

On Maui, we would get up about 3:00 A.M. and after a hearty drink of hot Ovaltine, we'd head out in Daisy's 1935 Ford and drive clear to the top of Haleakala hoping to see a glorious sunrise.

COLD!!! NEVER BEEN SO COLD!

One year Mother produced a half glass of whiskey for each of us and it helped to warm our opus (tummies), and it amazed me that my straight-laced Mother was suddenly a lot of fun!

Daisy and her daughter Lois completed our foursome. Lois was about as plain as a girl could be but she had impressive wit, spunk, good humor, and a lovely figure. We four were game for any adventure. On the way up the mountain it would sometimes be so foggy we couldn't see the road ahead (no white lines then), and Lois and I would hang our heads out the window of the car telling Daisy which way to turn, giggling all the time. We rented retired polo ponies from Haleakala Ranch and kept them in a little paddock next to the house. We galloped on the dusty pineapple roads with the horses excitedly farting mile after mile. Afterward we brushed them down and fed and watered them.

We lived and enjoyed every minute on Maui that summer of 1935. We had to heat our bathwater on the stove and then pour it into the bathtub. Most of the time the bathwater was lukewarm. Once we dove into the cistern with our bathing suits on and had a cool dip in our drinking-water supply. We caught heck for that.

We were staying in what was called the mountain house and it belonged to the Puunene Sugar Company. Aunt Daisy's husband, Ed Sabin, was the sugar mill engineer and had the privilege of borrowing the mountain house as well as the beach house at Spreklesville. The mountain house was up country from Makawao. There was the fragrance of eucalyptus mixed with pineapple and barnyard.

Haleakala Ranch was a renowned place owned by the Von Tempski family. Armine Von Tempski wrote the book *Born in Paradise*, which describes old Hawaii as the people with land, horses, and servants lived the dream. We lived the same dream, only on a much smaller scale.

Before I leave horses well enough alone, I must tell you about my first horseback ride. It occurred on the world famous Parker Ranch on the island of Hawaii, the year was 1926, and I was still just a little tyke not yet in school.

Growing Up

Mother wanted to visit a friend of hers who was the nurse for the ranch. We were to stay at the ranch.

We rode the little inter-island steamer, the *Humuulu,* fondly nicknamed the *Hula-Hula,* overnight to Kawaihai Harbor on the Big Island of Hawaii, where we were helped into a long boat and then rowed to the wharf. I remember it was chilly in the early morning, and I wore my little pale-blue wool coat lined in silk because I hated anything scratchy.

We stayed at the ranch headquarters, but the only part I remember is the birthday party where the main event at the party was a horseback ride. Several little kids were put on the back of a horse all at the same time and were being led around by one of the *paniolos,* the word for Hawaiian cowboys.

When it came my turn to be placed on the horse's back, I was at the rear end behind several other little tots. The next thing I knew the horse flung its back legs up and I went flying. They did not put me back on.

From then on I was very leary of horses.

Years later my mother's friend became pregnant and left the ranch. My mother was very sad about it, and that's when I learned that it's not a good thing to be pregnant and not married. Mother did not tell me this. I just kept my ears open and figured it out for myself.

CHAPTER 5

Living In Waikiki

"Centipedes are always long and always in a hurry."

Mother and Dad were part of the early-1900's generation, and they heard Galli-Curci and Caruso and Madame Schumann-Heink in person. Mother was in San Francisco the day that Schumann-Heink sang "The Last Rose of Summer" in front of Lotta's fountain on Market Street, and the part that was so marvelous was that the diva's glorious voice thrilled everyone all the way up and down Market Street.

And she didn't have a microphone!

Mom took me to hear Galli-Curci when the opera star was sailing from Honolulu on a ship in 1926. I remember it clearly even though I could not have been more than four. Galli-Curci's face was practically hidden by leis and she sang "Aloha Oe" from the deck as the ship began to pull away from the pier. It was a dramatic, unforgettable sight and sound, and later on Mother claimed I sang the music perfectly.

From then on I wanted to be an opera singer.

Mother had a lot of stories she liked to relate in order to get a laugh. There was the one about Betty saying to the iceman, "Dood morning. Close de door." I was sitting in the kitchen on the little white potty with my little knees sticking up and my little bottom getting red around the ring from sitting there so long. I was supposed to sit there until I *did* it, and I think I made up my mind that hell would freeze over before I would comply, since they made such an issue of it and embarrassed me in front of all their friends and the nice iceman.

We had a round icebox and the ice-man lifted the top lid and flung the ice in there. I needed some ice on my bottom is what I needed.

Another story I hated was the time someone asked me, "Where did you get your curly hair, little girl?" and I replied, "At the ten cent store."

I hated being the center of everyone's laughter, since I felt they were laughing at my expense.

Another one they liked to tell was the time I said hello to my big brother on the Punahou campus. Jack was in junior high when I was still in grammar school. This particular day I was thrilled to see him walking with his friends, but I heard him say to them, "There's my nuisance now!"

Mom thought that was hilarious, and she added it to her repertoire of funny stories about Betty.

In other respects she had a generous nature. She would regularly gather up clothes and toys and eventually my swing set and dolls and drive up to Kalihi Orphanage and drop off everything. She would also meet the boats that were on their way to the Orient and collect any stray nuns who were on their way to China and in Honolulu just for the day. Mom would drive them around the island and treat them to lunch and a swim at Mokuleia. She'd always offer them a glass of sherry, and sometimes they accepted that too.

All Mother's stories were repeated to entertain mainland visitors who came to dinner, and they were repeated too often for my comfort.

After I started first grade Mom began to have a flair for real estate, and since she didn't have a lazy bone in her body, she began to manage her own rental property and to dream about building her own building someday.

We already had the apartments on Saratoga Road and two small studio apartments next to our garage. Saratoga Road was and still is the next street over from Beach Walk.

She made friends with Mrs. Lemon, who was a Waikiki real estate lady. She also made friends with Roy Kelley, Waikiki's most famous and respected architect, who designed many of the hotels built in the Thirties and Forties. The Reef Hotel is one example. He designed the apartment building Mom built in 1936 on Kuhio Ave next to where the Kuhio Theater is now.

Mrs. Lemon, tall and skinny, always wore a hat and carried a huge handbag. She was my first encounter with a real estate lady. I didn't know then that eventually I too would be a real estate lady. She showed Mom property and probably contributed greatly to my mother's understanding of the wealth that could accumulate through the ownership of real estate.

Thankfully, Mabel Dyer had vision and was not afraid of hard work.

Our Waikiki house was on the corner of Kalakaua Avenue and Beach Walk. The front porch was on the *mauka* (mountain) side, and it caught the mountain breezes. It

Living In Waikiki

was painted buff with white trim and was in the Twenties bungalow style. We had to have it inspected and treated every year in case the termites had gotten started. It had been so well maintained that when the hotel was built on the property many years later, the house was picked up and moved to a lot on the other side of the island, where it still stands.

Mother had her bedroom on the main floor, and I always shared her room until after my brother left for Harvard. My father always slept in his own room, which was built on the top of the house. The stairway to it was steep, but once you were there, the windows were open on four sides and the breeze blew through, and you could get a glimpse of the ocean from the back windows.

Dad also had a half bath of his own. His razor strop hung on his bathroom door, and as a little kid I loved to watch him strop his razor and soap his face and then carefully and skillfully slide the long narrow straight-edge razor over his face and under his chin. He frequently came to the breakfast table with tiny bits of toilet paper stuck onto his face to stop the flow of blood.

I don't know what life was like in my friends' houses because we didn't talk so freely then about personal stuff. I never felt abused, but I think I felt very controlled and suppressed. When I was little, I had a Japanese nurse named Noboko who dressed me in a little kimono and took me to the beach every afternoon. I always felt at home on the sand at Waikiki. It was warm and the breeze was gentle, and there was lots to see. As far as I can tell, Waikiki in that regard is still the same. Later on, after Marney Bellows, my first friend, moved to Manoa Valley, I was left pretty much on my own except for one little girl who lived on Saratoga Road, and Mother said something I'll never forget.

"Why do you want to play with her? She's Jewish."

I still can't understand why Mother said that, because later on one of our best-friend families, the Baskers, was a mixed Jewish-Gentile couple.

All my life I have had Jewish friends.

I was not ever aware of racial prejudice or religious prejudice in our home. That is why I was so surprised when my mother didn't want me to play with the little girl who lived on Saratoga Road. I stuck by my friend and played dolls with her anyway.

I never saw the priest in our home either. My dad did not believe in entertaining the clergy. After Mass, he wanted to go straight home. Mom would walk over to the bake sale or stop to visit with a friend and Dad would get in the Buick and blare the horn and holler, "*Mabel!*" and she'd have to come running and get in the car. She'd be sputtering and furious, but it didn't do any good. We frequently drove home from church with everyone gritting their teeth.

When it rains in Hawaii it can rain *very* hard, and the sound on Dad's bedroom roof was deafeningly loud. The rats who inhabited our attic from time to time would get restless and set off the large traps in the attic. The wind would whistle and shriek, and the palm fronds on the coconut trees would brush against the house and the coconuts would crash onto the roof, making us jump with fright.

Later on, the coconut trees had twelve-inch tin bindings put on them, and that kept the rats from climbing up the

Living In Waikiki

trees and getting into the attic. As for the coconuts, there is a legend that no one has ever been bonged by a falling coconut.

My most traumatic experience as a child was the time my father hacked a centipede with the hatchet. We were sitting in the living room one evening and all of a sudden a seven-inch long centipede appeared from nowhere and hurried across the rug. Centipedes are always long and always in a big hurry. Mom and I screamed, and Pop ran out to get a weapon to kill the monster. When he got back, the thing had stopped in the middle of the rug. We held our breaths, afraid it would run away before we could kill it. Daddy who also looked alarmed, proceeded to strike it repeatedly with the hatchet.

To our dismay, the dismembered pieces ran in different directions. We screamed again at this frightening sight, and after a few more wiggles, all the pieces curled up and died. I was totally shaken up and unable to face the thought of ever having to deal with another one.

It happened years later at Mokuleia. Again it was night time and we saw one come hurrying across the living room. This time Dad sprayed it with Black Flag and swept it up into a dust pan while my mother muttered, "They always come in pairs."

Oh, swell.

My brother, on the other hand, used to play with centipedes. He and his friends who lived at the other end of Waikiki would remove the pincers and then have races to see whose centipede would come in first.

I must tell about sitting on my tricycle out in front of our house and saying hello to all the people who walked past.

Born and Raised in Waikiki

There were dozens of them because there were lots of apartments on Beach Walk, and the people who worked downtown in the offices liked to live near the beach. I would sit there with my brown eyes, my curls, and my dress with the matching bloomers, and I would say *hello* to each one after they got off the street car and were walking home after work. They were always nice and would say *hello* back to me.

Mother observed this and said to me one day, "Why do you say hello to all those people you don't know?" and another story was born because I answered, "Some I knows and some I don't knows."

This time, I loved the story.

Our yard man was Kimura, and I liked to watch him eat his lunch. Kimura sat on his haunches and I sat on my haunches and watched him use his chopstick. He brought his lunch in a stacked tin container. The rice was in one of the compartments and some vegetables in another of the compartments. He would drink his tea and would always pour a little tea over the rice as he finished, just to make sure that all the rice had been eaten. Never a grain left over. It all smelled so delicious, but he never offered me a taste.

Masa was our cleaning woman and laundress. She worked for us all the while I was growing up and kept the house clean and me in fresh clothes for many wonderful years. Masa lived in an enclave of little wooden Japanese-style houses with a bath house in the middle of the alley. It was over near where the University Theater is now.

Most of my friends had day servants like ours, but some of them had live-in maids and cooks and chauffeurs and

Living In Waikiki

yardmen. As I recall, we paid Masa fifteen dollars a week.

The popular fear back then was the dread of what would happen if *they* (the Orientals) took over. I remember Mother vividly expressing her opinion that we would all be, "slit from ear to ear."

She would make a dramatic swiping motion under her chin, and I would shudder.

We had several important business people in our lives. One was the pig farmer who picked up the slop bucket every week. That was our name for the wet garbage. The bucket was a ten-gallon can hung by a heavy wire. It had a wooden lid on it. It hung just outside the back screen door, and if I didn't like what I was being urged (forced) to eat, I would pretend I was going to eat it eventually, when actually my pre-set plan was to rush to the back door and flip it into the bucket. I'd out wait my parents, and they'd leave me at the breakfast-nook table, and when I figured it was safe, I'd make a mad dash to dump the canned peaches or the seedy tomatoes into the bucket. I knew if I didn't get rid of them I'd have to eat them at the next meal.

Another important person was the egg lady. She lived on a farm out at Waialae across the highway from where the golf course is and where there are million-dollar homes now. Mother, having grown up on a ranch, refused to buy eggs in the grocery store. The ones in the store were called mainland eggs, and goodness knows how many weeks it had been since the hen had laid them. After all, we had a mom who thought nothing of whipping up a gold cake with a dozen yolks or an angel food cake with a dozen egg whites. So we always needed an egg lady.

We had a Japanese man who drove a Model-T truck, and

every so often he would chug-chug into our long driveway and dump a load of chicken manure by the garage. It would still be steaming. Kimura used it in the yard and the flower beds. It was smelly and rich, and on a hot day the bees as well as the flies would be attracted to the pile. We had huge black bumblebees that would fly after you if you walked near it.

We had Japanese ladies who wandered all over Waikiki and other neighborhoods selling bunches of beautiful fresh flowers. One could hear their call from far away. *Frow. Frow.* They were Japan-born and could not say the L in flower, so it was *frow*. They usually wore blue and white cotton kimonos, and their long hair was twisted and piled on their head and held in place with long black hair pins. The baskets full of fresh red ginger, bird of paradise, gladioli and daisies and carnations and others were balanced on one shoulder and supported by a free hand: one dozen glads for one dollar, gardenias and daisies in bunches for twenty-five cents, bunches of gardenias for five cents.

The vegetable man had a flat-bed truck with shelves laden with lettuce, papayas, pineapples, carrots, apples, and other fruits and vegetables. One day the vegetable man was making his rounds in Waikiki, driving down the Ala Wai and my friend Betty McCuaig, who had just gotten her driver's license, lost control and drove her car into the wagon. Picture vegetables scattered all over the street and Meskie crying and laughing at the same time. She caught heck for that, but we loved to hear her tell the story.

It was convenient to have these independent business people come to our house in Waikiki. Each one had a horn or a whistle or a call of some kind to announce their arrival.

Living In Waikiki

While I was still pretty small, several traumatic events took place. The first was a multiple murder. A family of mother and father and three children lived in a little house on the beach end of Beach Walk. One day, the father hacked to death his wife and his children and then took his life. It was gruesome, and we all walked down the street and stared at the house where this had happened.

The second impressive event was a fire. The house that burned up was a large, two-story brown shingle house about halfway down Beach Walk on the Diamond Head side of the street. We heard the sirens and could see the smoke and smell and hear the crackling and smell the burning wood. Mother grabbed my hand, and with her heels clicking, we ran down the street to the scene of the blaze. The crowd gathered quickly, and the firemen could not contain the blaze, and we all stood numbly watching the whole house flame and crash.

The most memorable was a kidnapping and murder. A young boy attending Punahou was kidnapped. This was a monstrous and unheard-of crime for our islands, and a ghastly nightmare for the family and a very scary time for all the little children of Honolulu. A man disguised himself as a chauffeur and told the teacher on yard duty that he was there to pick up the little boy. The newspapers played it up and wrote that the kidnapper intended to snatch other children. It was perceived to be a vendetta of sorts against the Caucasian children. At any rate, many of us were kept at home while the police looked for the kidnapper.

Sadly, the little boy was found dead two days later, and his kidnapper was caught and executed. The motive for the crime was never decided, but from then on, if a person was picking up a child at Punahou School, a strict procedure was followed, and no one could pick up a child unless that person was known to the teacher as well as to the child, and the teacher had a note from the parents.

It was a very sobering and sad episode in Punahou history. It almost broke Miss Winne's heart. She was the principal of Bishop Hall, the grammar school of Punahou, and she was loved and respected. Her full name was Mary Persis Winne, but she was always called just Miss Winne. Her sister was named Jane, and we called her Miss Jane. Miss Winne was a comfortably large woman who always wore white dresses with a drop waist and belt of the same material, with white shoes and white stockings. She wore her long white hair streaked with gray piled up on the top of her head in a flat bun, kept in place with six-inch-long tortoise-shell hairpins. I remember that her hair always looked very clean and fluffy. She truly loved little children and was kind.

I was only called into her office once, in the fourth grade. I had been accused of lying. I don't remember what it was about. At any rate, my Mother was indignant, and she accompanied me to Miss Winne's office.

"Betty is not a liar."

I loved my Mother for coming with me and to my defense.

I loved singing, and Miss Jane was a good music teacher and taught us the traditional Hawaiian songs: "Aloha Oe," " Makalapua" and "Song of the Islands" plus lots of other favorites. She liked my voice and asked me to sing a duet with another second grader, Babbie Henshaw, at assembly.

When the day came, I had my share of stage fright but

Living In Waikiki

felt sustained by the thought that my friend would be there also. Well, my friend did not show up, and I had to do a solo. It was my first solo, but not my last. I was going to do a lot of singing in my life. Later on in fifth grade, I put raisins down Babbie's back to get even, and she squealed on me and got me in trouble, and I had to sit at a special desk next to the teacher. It was very embarrassing.

Punahou was experiencing changes and progressive educators were coming to the islands and heading for Punahou as soon as they got off the boat. They were eager to see if they could suggest changes to make Punahou School even better.

There I was in front of the whole class at a desk next to the teacher's. They all wanted to know, "What's that little girl doing up there sitting by herself?"

Of course the whole class laughed at me, and once again I wished I had polished Babbie off earlier. She was a very powerful little girl. Her daddy was a big-shot attorney, and mine owned a small store. Her mother was very social, and mine managed her own apartments and did much of the work. She lived in a gorgeous house near Oahu Country Club, and I lived in a very nice Waikiki two-story bungalow. She had a great beach house at Kailua, and I had an unfashionable beach house at Mokuleia. She had power.

She knew how to use it, and I was afraid to challenge her. Probably just as well, since we went to school together for the rest of the time, and I spent many marvelous weekends at her Kailua house and went to terrific parties at her house in town when we were all sophisticated teenagers. The Henshaws were the epitome of Hawaiian hospitality,

Born and Raised in Waikiki

and I greatly admired their style of living.
   It was exactly what I wanted when I grew up.

CHAPTER 6

The Dole Derby

"Martin, where in the hell have you been?"

My mother was always a sport when it came to being where things were happening, and so she and I drove out to Wheeler Field on the plains of Schofield on Oahu early one morning in 1927.

Charles Lindbergh had made history by flying solo across the Atlantic that same year, and so a prize-winning race was announced for flyers to solo across the Pacific from Oakland, California, to Wheeler Field on Oahu. They called it the Dole Derby, and seven pilots entered the race. First-place winner would receive $25,000, and second-place $10,000.

Many years later, in 1941, the Japanese would bomb and strafe Wheeler Field on December 7th. But this day in 1927 was going to be a joyous day for the pilot who got there first and won all that dough.

There were bleachers set up alongside the field facing in the direction of the faintly visible Diamond Head. The planes would have to fly around that famous landmark on their way to Wheeler Field. The bleachers were filled with officers in their splendid uniforms and their ladies equally dolled up for the occasion. The ladies held the sun off with parasols.

Mom and I were part of the crowd standing next to the bleachers. I had on my sailor *mokus* (pants) and a little sweater to ward off the chill of the early morning. As the morning dragged on Mom bought me a shave ice. The shave ice carts had a tool that looked like a carpenter's plane, but instead of wood, it shaved off the ice from a large block of ice. On top of the cupful of ice, they poured a strawberry, cherry, or pineapple syrup and the price was a nickle.

Meanwhile, all eyes were straining to see the planes when they would come around Diamond Head. The radio stations and the newspapers and cameramen were there as well as a military band playing lively music. I was filled with suspense and impatience.

It seemed hours later when someone shouted, "Here they come!"

We could see a black dot coming around Diamond Head that slowly got bigger and bigger and finally became a small-single engine airplane.

When it landed, we all cheered and screamed, and the band played even louder.

The winner, Art Goebel, got out of his plane, the *Woolaroo*, and we applauded wildly. The second and last of the arrivals was Martin Jensen in his Breese monoplane *Aloha*. Jensen was a Honolulu pilot and so he had a lei painted around the nose of his plane as well as the Territory of Hawaii seal on the fuselage sides. He signed up for the race and advertised for a navigator and received three replies; from a fourteen-year-old Boy Scout, a 16-year-old

The Dole Derby

movie starlet, and from Navy navigator Paul Schluter.

After twenty-eight hours in the air from California to Wheeler Field, his wife, whom he had married on the wings of a biplane over Yuma, Arizona, greeted him with, *"MARTIN, WHERE IN THE HELL HAVE YOU BEEN?"*

Five contestants had disappeared over the Pacific. Martin Jensen continued his aviation career, lived a long life, and is enshrined in the Pioneers of Aviation Hall of Fame at the San Diego California Aerospace Museum.

Commercial aviation began between the mainland of California and Honolulu and the Orient in 1935. The first flight was the Pan-American Oriental Clipper commanded by Captain Edwin Musick. The elapsed time was just under nineteen hours. Today in jet airplanes the flight is five hours or less depending on the winds. Mother's friend, Clara, had a husband who often went on buying trips to the states. Frequently there would be mechanical problems, and the plane would return to Honolulu. So the *point of no return* was halfway across the Pacific. Those left behind in Honolulu counted the hours until they were certain the plane would not be returning for repairs.

As I said, my mother was always a sport about being where things were happening. In the late 1930's when Babe Ruth was on a world tour, he stopped in Honolulu for an exhibition game. I was dying to go and when I called home to get permission to be late coming home from school there was no answer. So I decided to chance it and to go to the game anyway. You guessed it. I got to the game and there was my mother! And the Babe hit a homer too.

CHAPTER 7

My First Trip to The Mainland

..."too tall to be a flower girl."

In 1929, when I was seven years old, I was chosen to play the part of Peter Pan in the school play. I was thrilled to have been chosen out of all the school, and when I asked Mother if I could do it, she said I would have to turn it down because we were going to visit my aunt Laura and to Seattle to attend my mother's friend's daughter's wedding. I was to be a flower girl. Being a flower girl didn't measure up to being in the Punahou play but I had no power over my own life then and so off we went on my first trip to the Mainland. We went by boat.

In June of 1929, Jack, Mother and myself sailed on the *Wilhelmina* and that is where we met Aunt Daisy Sabin from Maui traveling with her seven-year-old daughter, Lois. I was still mad at mother for dragging me away, and I got even more put out with her because she made me dance the hula for a lot of strangers who were also on the ship. Mom and I had taken hula lessons from a petty tyrant named Mrs. Neff. We learned together. We shook our fingers and wrists to limber up our hands and make them more graceful, and we learned to dance "Lili-u-e,"

My First Trip to The Mainland

the hula for Liliuokalani, Hawaii's last Queen. Her Majesty had been deposed in 1893, and while she was in house arrest, she composed Hawaii's most beloved song, "Aloha Oe."

I was always embarrassed whenever my mother would jump up and do the hula, and I was mad as heck when she'd push me into doing it at her bidding. Outside of that, the trip was fun, and I was happy to discover that I was a good sailor. Lois and I became buddies and played cards incessantly and ate everything in sight while our mothers lay groaning in their bunks.

We docked in Portland, Oregon, after going up the Columbia River. It all looked like a foreign country to my palm-tree, rolling-surf eyes. The air smelled funny too. No flowers and lots of redwood and pine smells. We drove our Buick to Seattle after it was unloaded from the boat.

Aunt Laura lived in Seattle on East 59th Street in a neighborhood of nice two-story white houses. Uncle Will, her husband, worked for the Fisher Flour Mill. The popcorn man came tooting and whistling around in the evening, and I fell madly in love with a nine-year-old boy. Falling madly in love meant that I thought about him a lot, but we never kissed or anything. I think he chased me around a couple of bushes a couple of times. I was thrilled.

During this visit to Seattle in 1929, when I was supposed to be a flower girl, I experienced the first rejection of my life. We drove to the church for the rehearsal. I was excited and finally feeling happy about being in a wedding. I met the bride and her mother and then I was led to a seat at the back of the church. It was dark there, and I could hear whispering and see looks in my direction. Pretty soon my mother came back with the news that I was too tall to be a flower girl.

I remember how my skin felt, how my throat felt, how my head swirled, and how I wanted to die. I was angry, humiliated, and powerless to do anything about it.

I always thought my Mother should have stood up for me and said something like, "Look here, I took Betty away from her chance to be in the Punahou play and you simply can't do this. You will have to have her be a junior bridesmaid or something equally impressive."

But of course, she didn't, and who could? But I sure as hell never forgot it, and anytime she talked about her friend and her friend's daughter, I always blanked my ears and didn't listen.

We rented a cottage at Lake Wilderness near Seattle. We had a small row boat, and I was allowed to be on the lake in the boat rowing myself around because I could swim. We fished for crappies, hauled in crayfish, went down a huge slide, and played the juke box at the little headquarters for the lake. The popular songs were "Ninety-nine Out of a Hundred Want to be Kissed" and "I'm in Love with You, Honey."

We drove to Mt. Rainier for Jack's thirteenth birthday. My dad had sent us each five dollars and in addition told my mother to give Jack a birthday he would never forget. So we drove up to see the snow, and on the way back that Sunday night in August 1929, Mother was sideswiped by a car passing us and we ended up turned over in the ditch. I was asleep when it happened. The car, with us in it, got hauled to a hospital in Tacoma.

Several hours later, we finally got home to Aunt Laura's

My First Trip to The Mainland

house, shakenup but not hurt. I have never slept in a car since then.

During that same summer of 1929, we drove our Buick from Seattle to San Francisco, Mom in the front seat driving, Aunt Laura alongside her, and Jack and I warring in the back seat. Jack constantly took jabs at me with his knuckles. I slugged him with my drinking cup. I hit him on the temple one time, and I was told that since I hit his temple I might have killed him. That was impressive but I wasn't sorry.

The back seat was a war zone, but Mom and Laura were in their own world. We hauled up to a stop whenever we spotted a sign advertising farm produce. Consequently it was not unusual for Aunt Laura to be stringing beans or shelling peas as we rolled along at thirty-five miles an hour.

We stayed at motels, called auto courts, and of course each cottage had a sink and little gas range. And maybe an ice box too.

One day I experienced another form of rejection. We were driving past a lovely cool-looking spot with cabins and a large slide and swimming pool on the river with lots of large shade trees too. It looked ideal for us. Mom pulled off the highway and the proprietor walked up to look us over. She eyed our Hawaii license plate and then she eyed me with my usual dark tan, and she snapped out, "We don't take niggers."

Mother was outraged!

That was another story Mom told over and over. It was slightly funny, and this time I could see the humor in it.

We stopped off in Willows, California, to search out

Born and Raised in Waikiki

Mom's birthplace. When we finally found it, the place was about to collapse, and the sheep had been running through it for years. Mom laughed, but I felt a sense of disappointment. I was hoping to find a large mansion that I could be proud of.

We drove into San Francisco in July, 1929, and stayed at a little hotel on Market Street. San Francisco was having a heat wave. I still had my five from Dad, plus another five he sent me because I had written him a letter betting him five dollars that I loved him. Another favorite story. Jack was griped that he hadn't thought of it too. It made up for all the jabs I had endured in the back seat.

We went to dinner at an Italian place which had sawdust on the floor. I remarked to the waiter that the black olives were *rotten* and he daggered me with, "Not rotten, little girl. *RIPE!*"

When we went home on the boat at the end of summer, we took our car home with us. Mom had bought at least twenty new hats and lots of shoes, size seven AAAA. All purchases were stuffed into the car. My first trip to the mainland was over.

It had been wonderful.

CHAPTER 8

Magical Waikiki

"One family from Chicago even brought a French maid."

Waking up in Waikiki is waking up in the tropics. The Hawaiian Islands sit out in the Pacific Ocean all by themselves. They are roughly 2200 miles from the coast of California and Mexico and between 18 and 22 degrees north of the Equator. They were discovered by Captain James Cook in 1778. He claimed them for England and that is why the Hawaiian flag is similar to the British Union Jack.

Before one is fully awake one becomes aware of the sounds: usually the doves coo-coo-cooing and very often the mynah birds making a terrible din with their constant screeching and squawking. Usually there is a breeze, and you can hear the palm fronds swishing back and forth. If you are lucky, you can hear the sound of the waves as they come onto the shore. In the winter when the ocean is heavier and more insistent, you can hear the waves as they hammer and crash onto the distant reef.

As the morning waxes, the other birds begin to talk to each other. The cardinals from Brazil add their voices. They were imported during the Thirties so that Hawaii would have beautiful birds again. So many of the older species had died out when the magnificent feather cloaks and leis were made for the royal Hawaiians.

Memories of Waikiki in those days, the Twenties and the Thirties, are unique. For one thing, we Waikiki kids always had streetcars, and we rode them most of the time. We also had hotels, stores, and taverns nearby. The old streetcars were very familiar to me because as a tiny child I used to have a long Sunday, afternoon ride with Noboko. She and I would get ourselves up the side steps and settle ourselves on the slippery wooden seat and ride all the way from Waikiki to Fort Shafter and back for a nickel each way.

The cars were open on all sides, and one could enter anywhere on the side where there was a vacant seat. I feel as if I grew up on streetcars and buses with the breezes blowing clear through. They clanged their way along Kalakaua Avenue as far as the zoo at the Diamond Head end of Waikiki. Since the noisy streetcars went right past our house, sometimes we couldn't hear what the other person was saying in our own living room.

When the Outrigger Canoe Club was next to the Royal Hawaiian Hotel, one could see the famous surfboards and their owners. The boards were huge monolithic things made of koa wood or redwood. It took a real man to heft one on to his shoulder and walk or trot to the water's edge, whomp it into the ocean, and then hop on the board, all in one fluid motion. The boards each had a name carved into them.

The owners stood them on end in front of the club. Duke Kahanamoku's board was named *DUKE*. It was not uncommon to see him standing on the beach by the club. In

Magical Waikiki

1912, Duke Kahanamoku smashed all world swimming records at the Summer Olympics in Stockholm, Sweden. He was 22 years old, a full-blooded Hawaiian standing 6 feet 2 inches tall, and believe it or not, he had never been in a pool! He had done all his training in the ocean.

If you go to Waikiki now, you can see a statue of Duke. It is lifesized and in bronze. He is standing next to his board facing Kalakaua Avenue with his back to the ocean. The local people objected to the positioning, because, as they said, the Duke would never have stood with his back to the ocean. Bad luck!

The canoes were also objects of admiration. Each had its own name, and each one had its own resting place of honor. Every canoe and board was poised and ready for fun. It was a thrill to see Duke Kahanamoku and his brother Sergeant and Chick Daniels and also Dad Center and the rest of the *beach boys*. I used to see Gay Harris at church too. And Dad Center was already getting gray, but he gave me swimming lessons.

A major activity for some of the beach boys besides surfing and canoeing and giving lessons and playing the uke was weaving lauhala hats and rubbing coconut oil onto the backs of the pretty female tourists. Everyone tried to get a terrific tan. The darker the better. The air reeked of coconut oil.

Water wings were the swimmies of that time. With a strip of cloth in between, the wings would get blown up, and then the strip would support you in the water.

Ladies wore dark wool bathing suits with matching dark black wool underpants attached to the suit. No lady would think of going into the water without an elaborate system of chamois strips wrapped around the head, followed by a rubber bathing cap, all designed to keep the hair dry. We usually wore bathing shoes too. Waikiki has always had loose pieces of coral to cut the feet.

One more thing must be remembered about Waikiki in the early days. A woman could be arrested and fined if she walked on the sidewalks in a bathing suit without a cover-up that came at least to her knees. I mean she *had* to wear a robe or jacket. It was the law. Boy, have things changed, or what?

Speaking of the Royal Hawaiian, my mother and dad went to the grand opening in 1927. Mother wore a clinging crepe evening gown in a light salmon color. Her dark eyes sparkled like the rope of crystal beads she wore with crystal drop earrings. Her perfume was always Black Narcissus. Her figure was hourglass, and need I add, she looked ravishing. My dad was in his tuxedo and looked very proud and happy.

The clinging crepe dress did not have another outing until much later when Mother made me wear it to a teenage party on Maui. Of course, I looked ridiculous in it, and I remember being embarrassed and having a lousy time. No one explained to me that we were cutting back due to the Depression.

The Moana Hotel was on the beach at Waikiki before the Royal. It had cottages as well as the hotel building. Near the cottages, which were across the street from the hotel, were six tennis courts. My dad played there every Sunday morning. The Banyan court of the hotel was the site of *Hawaii Calls*, a radio broadcast which was hosted by Webley Edwards for many, many years.

Magical Waikiki

Thousands of tourists were drawn to dream of coming to Waikiki after listening to the music of *Hawaii Calls*, Webley would take the microphone to the water's edge, and millions of people would hear the sound of the waves coming onto the shore. I'd hear that later on when I was away at college, and I'd get homesick.

A block away from the Moana Hotel on a small side street was the former home of Princess Kaiulani. The home was called Aina Hau, place of the Hau tree. Mother would drive me by the gate, and then we'd peer in through the overgrown trees and shrubs, and she would talk about how Robert Louis Stevenson visited the Princess there at one time. The house was still standing, and it seemed to be single story with a large lanai (porch) along the front. By the time I was made aware of it, it was deserted. The princess died in her early twenties, and there was a sadness about the place. You can see her portrait in the Princess Kaiulani Hotel.

The fun part of growing up was living close to Waikiki beach and getting to go there by myself or with a girl friend. When we got to be older, we were admonished to never talk to strangers, particularly soldiers. They were young men who needed a job during the Depression, and the Army offered work, a home and three meals a day.

I remember how those poor homesick guys would approach us young island girls and try to talk to us. We'd rebuff them, and they'd take it good-naturedly and walk away. Many of them wore bathing suits that revealed the dimensions of their private parts. We girls thought those kind of bathing suits were disgusting. We called them soldier suits.

Born and Raised in Waikiki

Waikiki comprises a total of one hundred and eighty one acres, and yet it pays more property taxes than all the sugar land and pineapple land and ranch land in the state. Kalakaua Avenue is still the main thoroughfare in Waikiki. It was named for King Kalakaua, who was known as the Merry Monarch because he loved to gamble and to party. His sister was Queen Liliuokalani, Lily of Heaven.

Across the street from our house, on the corner of Beach Walk and Kalakaua Avenue, was a large swampy area known as the duck ponds. It was a several block area consisting of coral with water on the surface. It was whitish from the coral. We could dig down in our own back yard and reach the water level in less than two feet.

Once in a while we would get heavy rains, and our back yard would be flooded with one to two feet of water. I remember having fun with my brother sailing little homemade boats in our yard. When the Ala Wai Canal was built in the Twenties, it effectively drained Waikiki and dirt was brought in and put over the coral base and lots for houses were created.

Our house on Beach Walk was on fee-simple property, but many of the lots along the Ala Wai as well as other streets in Waikiki are on leased land. People who live on leased land pay lease rent to the owner of the fee title. In this way much of the land in Hawaii has remained in the hands of the original owners, whose descendants enjoy the lease income. Some of the leased land estates are thousands of acres with hundreds of houses or other types of buildings. Each individual user pays lease rent to the fee title owner. This is in addition to whatever home mortgage payments exist on the individual lots. The real wealth in

Magical Waikiki

Hawaii has always been in the ownership of land. Many of the largest estates acquired their land from the early kings and queens, either by marrying the current princess or, close relative of royalty. Sometimes land was acquired as payment for a gambling debt.

In the old days if the landowner wanted to keep people from trespassing over his property he would nail up a sign that said *KAPU*. We all knew it meant *KEEP OUT*, but the tourists didn't know that. So it was *KAPU* here and *KAPU* there all over the island, and some of the tourists wondered who this Mr. Kapu was who owned so much land.

Some time in the Thirties, Doris Duke, the tobacco heiress, had a small mansion built out at Diamond Head and she wanted to fence off the beach from the locals. This confrontation ended when the courts declared, once-and-for-all, that the beaches in Hawaii belong to all the people of Hawaii.

The Waikiki of my growing-up years in the 1920's and 30's consisted of the Moana Hotel, the Halekulani Hotel, the Royal Hawaiian Hotel and the Niumalu Hotel, plus several boarding-type hotels and many small cottages. Wealthy tourists came out from Chicago and other snowy areas to spend the winter. Some even brought their own car and their own driver, and maid. It was the talk of the town when one family from Chicago even brought a French maid.

In Waikiki we lived side-by-side with various businesses. Our service station, where we bought gas for twenty-five cents a gallon, was only one block away. The Piggly Wiggly grocery store was three blocks away. It had the first shopping carts in Honolulu. Dairyman's Ice

Cream was next to the grocery. Lau Yee Chai's marvelous Chinese restaurant, irreverently referred to as Lousy Chai's, was across the street from Dairyman's. I would often walk my dog Kam to Dairyman's and buy him an ice cream cone for a nickel.

Beach Walk was never Beach Walk Street or Avenue. It is, was, and always has been just plain Beach Walk. Beach Walk is a one-block street. It starts at Kalakaua Avenue and curves down past a few small hotels and restaurants and car rental places and ends at Kalia Road which is the road that runs parallel to the ocean. So you see, if you want to get to the ocean, you simply walk down Beach Walk, cross Kalia Road, and then go down the right-of-way to the beach and *Aloha*! There is Waikiki Beach and Diamond Head.

We had the darndest Christmas trees in the Twenties and Thirties. They were shipped from Washington and Oregon after having been cut in late October. After two weeks on the boat and a week or so on the docks, they were ready for the Christmas tree lot by early December. Usually the needles were dangerously close to falling off by the time we had the tree up in the living room. The pine fragrance was gone.

During the war we did not get any trees shipped down to us, and so Mother asked Kimura to haul in the Fan Palm tree that grew in a large cement pot. We decorated it and hung lights on it and put it in the front windows where passersby could see it. Dozens of men in uniform walked down Kalakaua Avenue and stopped to gaze at the tree. Many would be wiping their cheeks as they stood there.

That year, 1944, Bing Crosby sang Irving Berlin's new

Magical Waikiki

song, "White Christmas," and we talked about inviting the servicemen in, but we never did. There were too many of them.

Christmas Eve was really special in Waikiki. The houses, hotels, and stores were lit with Christmas lights and the beaches were packed with tourists escaping the cold. Not too much different from now, actually.

In those days the rich tourists spent the winter in Honolulu, and the schoolteachers and the college kids spent the summers. The winter tourists were my father's best customers.

We never opened our presents until after Mass at midnight, unless it was a very special present such as the year my dad gave me a fox fur. It was a reddish fox with little paws and a hand-crocheted fastener with a large snap. I put it around my shoulders and felt like a princess. It was probably seventy degrees outside, but by golly, it was Christmas, and I wore that fox fur to midnight Mass and hoped that all eyes were watching me.

They probably were!

Another time I received a string of real pearls. I had asked for department store pearls and had expected to get some nice fake pearls. Instead Daddy handed me a flat red leather packet about four inches by ten inches, and I gasped when I saw a strand of pearls held in place by a red leather strap. They were genuine Mikimoto pearls from Japan.

Boy, was I *surprised* and thrilled down to my bobby socks. I was beginning to feel as if I was pretty special, and the lovely glow the pearls made around my neck let me feel pretty at last. I didn't have any dates, but I was getting all the girl things that I knew would make me attractive.

We left for St. Augustine's at Waikiki in time to be in our pew by 11:30 P.M. The Hawaiian choir would sing before Mass, and the crowds would pour in and the aisle would be lined with extra seats. The soloist would sing "O, Holy Night" and my mother would practically swoon over his gorgeous voice.

One year I was asked to play the organ for the Christmas music. I had been taking piano lessons for at least five years, and so, nothing ventured, nothing gained. I got up to the choir loft and without practicing ahead of time, I plunged into the first hymn.

It sounded DREADFUL!

"Omigod!" I suddenly realized I was playing it in one sharp instead of one flat. Too late. The choir struggled through it and I pulled myself together enough to finish the hymns.

They never asked me again.

After Mass, we went home and finally we got to open all our presents. Daddy was in his element. He'd sit there and say, "Well, let's see what the super salesman sold."

We could have killed him. Aunt Sadie always mailed over her Christmas rocks (cookies), and Aunt Laura always sent jars of her blackberry jelly. Aunt Lot usually sent Olde Spice and something she had gotten with coupons, and Aunt Nell always sent rosaries and holy cards.

Then the best part of Christmas Eve happened. We gradually realized that we could hear Christmas music, and we knew that the Hawaiian boys were serenading us, once more singing in lovely harmony. The night was dark and the sky was filled with stars and the air was warm and

Magical Waikiki

flower scented, and the music filled us with peace. "Silent Night," "O Come all Ye Faithful"—Hawaiian style.

After the serenade, Mother made a delicious breakfast. We had been enjoying egg nog all during the unwrapping. And we had fun running Jack's train, which had been set up in the living room. By three o'clock in the morning, we were tired out and ready to hit the hay, grateful that we didn't have to go to church again in the morning.

Christmas Day was sunny and warm, naturally, and I would skate down Beach Walk to my friend Meskie's house so we could tell each other what we got for Christmas. This visit might be followed by a nice swim. After all, the ocean was always there to welcome us. It didn't usually rain until January and even so we loved to swim in the warm rain. Rain was like having an outside shower.

New Year's Eve was always INCREDIBLE MASSES OF INDISCRIMINATE NOISE! Firecrackers in long streamers were exploding all over town! People would hang over the balconies of hotels and drop whole strings of firecrackers onto the ground beneath. It was chaotic and dangerous.

One year my friend Ethelwynne Lewis's house on Diamond Head burned to the ground, and all her family's valuable and priceless Koa wood calabashes were lost in the fire, all because of firecrackers.

CHAPTER 9

Getting Older

"Edward, the Prince of Wales, played with them in the Thirties."

Mother signed me up for ukulele lessons. I was not thrilled, but I was not against it either. By this time I was about twelve, and I could walk to my lessons by myself. The teacher's name was Mr. Diamond. He could play the uke better than anyone I've ever heard. His studio was on a side street down by Kuhio Beach where Duke Kahanamoku's bronze statue now stands. At that time the Steiner house and the houses next to it were still lived in by the owners. They were on the Diamond Head side of the Moana Hotel, right by the ocean.

Waikiki Tavern was practically across the street from my lesson site. I loved to peer inside the tavern and wonder at the laughter I could hear. I could see clear through the tavern to the sparkling blue ocean, and I could see the grown-ups inside dancing and sitting around having fun. It fascinated me.

Each island back then, in the Twenties and Thirties, had several really influential families. Some were descendants of missionaries and others were the descendants of adventuresome people who had settled in Hawaii in the early

Getting Older

days. John Palmer Parker, the founder of Parker Ranch, went to the Big Island (Hawaii) on a sailing ship in the last half of the 19th century. He became a friend of King Kamehameha the Great and married the king's granddaughter and founded a dynasty of hardworking and fun-loving *hapa-haoles* (part Hawaiians), many of whom were at Punahou with me and can claim to have royal blood.

In the 1930's when there would be polo every Sunday at Kapiolani Park, I would drive there with my pals and try not to stare at the women who smoked their cigarettes in long holders, wore beautiful white linen dresses, gold jewelry or pearls, and dashed everything off with dark glasses and silk scarves. This spelled *GLAMOUR!*

One of my secret idols was Jimmy Castle. He must have been in his early thirties, a bachelor and so handsome and watchable. He drove a 1936 Ford touring car, usually with the top down. When he drove through Waikiki, all heads turned. Naturally he played polo on the Oahu team. Edward, the Prince of Wales, played with them once in the Twenties.

Occasionally we would be invited to sit with the glamorous women in the canopied stand on the chairs covered in heavy white cotton and breathe their perfume and listen to their chatter and begin to think there was a great big fascinating world waiting for grown-up girls.

There was Chiquita Winn and her husband, Montgomery Clark. Were there ever any names so intrinsically glamorous? She looked like Dolores Del Rio, dark hair slicked back and gold earrings and heavy gold bracelets and probably a white linen dress, impeccably tailored. It was the Duchess of Windsor look but all her own and long

Born and Raised in Waikiki

before the world had heard of Wallis Simpson. Her husband was sandy-haired and tanned and handsome in a light hearted way. Were these the Honolulu version of Jay Gatsby and his crowd?

These people all seemed to be born to ride horses. So naturally I took riding lessons along with my friends and had britches made at Linn's and bought some beautiful boots and learned how to jump my horse and all that.

I was eventually invited to a riding party at Waimanalo Ranch. Oodles of elegant riders were sitting comfortably on their horses. I was gripped by the icy fear of failure and could hardly mount my horse, whose ears were twitching back and forth. I knew that twitching was a bad sign.

Two hours later after galloping like maniacs all over Waimanalo Ranch, I managed to somehow get myself away from this insane crowd of horse-lovers and back to the familiar safety of Waikiki, where I belonged.

Travel between the islands before air travel emerged was an adventure. Nowadays, everyone climbs on and off airplanes as though the plane were a bus. Before the airplanes, the way to get from one island to another was by ship, always called *the boat*. The boats rolled and rattled and groaned their way between Honolulu and Hilo or Kahului or Kawaihai or Nawiliwili. It was great fun, and we kids who traveled to vacation places or to go home, seldom went to bed till early morning. We stayed up playing cards and eating delicious little chicken sandwiches that the willing stewards provided. One could go on deck and hear guitars and singing from the deck passengers. Sometimes we all joined in along with the chickens and the cattle.

One year I was lucky to get to go to camp on Kauai. I

Getting Older

loved everything about camp. We had gotten there by boat, of course, overnight from Honolulu to Nawiliwili Harbor on Kauai. We were a very large group, and so we slept on deck on three-inch-thick mattresses with army blankets, which did their best to keep us warm. We slept in our clothes. I just remember that the trip was chilly, the sky was lit up with millions of stars, and the music from guitars drifted out over the rolling sea. And at sea there were no mosquitoes.

It had been a boys' YMCA camp, and it got turned into a girls' camp for two weeks. I remember there were no seats on the toilets when we got there. The camp was on the beach near Haena. There were cabins that accommodated six campers in bunk beds. Bliss to be on my own, almost. I learned about K.P. duty and about eating camp food and the utter joy of everyone singing with meals. So different from my own home table, where we definitely did not sing!

We took day trips, and one of them was on a huge sampan owned by a Hawaiian named Hanohano. Hanohano and his large family lived in Hanalei. He and his deck hands transported at least thirty of us excited young teenagers on a ride down the dramatic Napali coast of Kauai.

We anchored off shore by the entrance to Kalalau Valley, and then the Hawaiian crew swam ashore and anchored a large rope in the sand and we went hand over hand from the boat to the shore. Talk about exciting! After we were all safely on shore, we explored the cave and walked a short way into the valley, where we found a waterfall just our size. It was actually a nice stream that tumbled down over some smooth rocks, and it was a perfect place to slip around and shriek and wash off the salt water and sand.

Breakfast was cooked on individual stoves we made out of coffee cans that we upended. We made a fire underneath the can and cooked on the bottom of the can. It worked just great, and we had bacon and eggs. We slept all night in the gigantic dry cave. The *pokani* (ghosts) were out in full force, and we told ghost stories and lay awake for hours listening and peering into the darkness. The surf finally coaxed us to sleep.

Hanohano came to pick us up the next day, and we hand-over-handed back to his boat. I felt *junk* (queasy) on the two hour ride home back to Hanalei.

Another milestone on this camp adventure was getting my Lifesaver Certificate. It seemed fairly harmless and worthwhile. I learned the "arm lock" and the "hair pull," and then went for the final test. Everyone had to have a partner, so you could be either the one pretending to drown or the one doing the rescuing.

I looked at my partner, and she turned out to be a very muscular Hawaiian *wahine* (girl). She gave me the *stink eye* and when she rescued me she darn near drowned me. When it was my turn to rescue her, I put on the head lock and prayed I could haul her in without drowning both of us. I got her safely to shore, and we both earned our badges. I was awfully proud of mine.

It meant recognition from someone other than my parents.

In the Thirties, there were no buildings obscuring the wonderful view of Diamond Head from the shores of Waikiki Beach. One could see the fabulous Castle white-

Getting Older

wedding-cake mansion built on the tip of Diamond Head by the ocean. Here and there one could see through the trees glimpses of the houses built on the slopes of Diamond Head, which is sometimes called Kaimana Hila.

Sometime during the Twenties, the Elks acquired the magnificent Castle landmark and used it for their clubhouse. It had been built partly over the water, and one could sit in the former spacious sun porch, now used as the dining room, and hear the water swishing underneath, and through the glass windows see the entire shoreline of Waikiki. The enormous ballroom was lined with mammoth floor-to-ceiling mirrors framed with ornate gold frames. Everywhere you glanced your reflection glanced back. It only needed a Viennese orchestra playing Strauss waltzes to complete the fantasy.

The ceilings were suitably high and as one swept up the wide steps from the porte cochere into the huge ballroom, one could imagine the fabulous parties for the Prince of Wales and other nobility who visited Hawaii, as well as parties for Hawaiian royalty.

After the war the beautiful mansion was torn down by the Elks, and a modern clubhouse built in its place. Sadly, the reminder of the glorious days of Waikiki's past is gone forever.

After the war, from 1946 on to the present, the hotels and condominiums that rose near Kaimana Hila threatened to obscure Diamond Head from view, and so a law was passed restricting building along the shore of Diamond Head. Before the law was passed, the Colony Surf Hotel and the Kaimana Hotel were built, along with several condominium projects, but lucky for all of us one can still see

Born and Raised in Waikiki

Diamond Head from Waikiki Beach

The Hawaiians called it Leahi. In the old days the way to communicate between islands was to build a huge fire and make smoke signals. Oahu built its fire on Diamond Head and thus it became known as Leahi, the fire.

In the Thirties and earlier, there were a few simply marvelous beach houses in between the Royal Hawaiian Hotel and the Halekulani Hotel. One of the houses was the Wilder house. There were usually ladies in white dresses and large straw hats sitting on the veranda looking out to sea.

The sea wall in front of these houses had a right of way along the top, and I stole looks at the front porches as I walked along the sea wall. First I ogled the tourists at the Halekulani, and then I ogled the beautiful people sitting on their *lanais*.

Tourists and locals and the soldiers from Fort De Russy even today walk along the top of the sea wall and look at the people on the other side of the fence. And the people inside the fence are people-watching right back at all the weird and wonderful bathing suits strutting, strolling, or jogging by. The trees still recognize me when I pass, and I always say hello to them and nod my respects.

The author Jack London and his wife Charmian lived in Waikiki and loved the islands so much. Their little rented house was on Beach Walk down near the beach. Mother and Dad used to see them swimming way out beyond the reef. As far as Mother was concerned, they were *very daring*.

My friends and I later discovered the same deep-water channel about a couple of hundred yards out in front of the Royal Hawaiian Hotel. We'd swim out there, locate the

Getting Older

clear channel, and then swim the length of the channel to where the Fort De Russy beach is today. It was a long swim and we'd have to float and rest on top of the water from time to time.

There is also a sand bar in front of the Royal Hawaiian Hotel dining room. One can swim out about a hundred yards and then feel for the sand bar and stand up in three feet of water.

I have seen Waikiki Beach with the water coming in large waves clear up to the sea wall at the Royal Hawaiian Hotel in the winter, with hardly any beach to lie on in front of the hotel. Later on, sand was imported and the beach was much improved, but Waikiki Beach has always had rather opaque water.

CHAPTER 10

Mokuleia Beach

"No one was in the house when the ferocious wave hit."

The same summer that I went to Ohio (1933), my uncle Wilfred de Jarlais, Mom's brother, and Walter Tanabe, a contractor from Waialua, had with Mother's direction built a basically one-room beach house at Mokuleia Beach on the North Shore of Oahu. She and Dad had bought in 1929, the smallest lot in the tract, Lot #33 on Crozier Drive. It was in the center of the tract and had a reliable water supply. The Mendonca family subdivided the tract and supplied the water.

I remember driving out to Mokuleia one Sunday when I was about five and having a very uncomfortable picnic next to the railroad tracks under the ironwood trees. We couldn't picnic on our lot because as yet it did not have any shade. Mother was thrilled to have the lot but Dad was noncommittal. He was basically a *city guy* as Mom called him, and it took him many years to get warmed up to the country.

Mother's brother Wilfred and his wife, Auntie Clara, and son, Billy, had been brought to live in Honolulu during the Depression. Mother had Uncle Wilfred to keep em-

Mokuleia Beach

ployed, and so she conceived the idea of building a beach house with his help and the help of the contractor.

They poured the slab for the floor, and after it was cured they raised a huge tent over the slab. We moved in a coal oil cookstove, an ice box, and several iron cots with mattresses and mosquito netting. At night the hum of the frustrated mosquitoes and the sound of the surf lulled us to sleep.

In the morning the train would hustle by on its way to Kahuku to load pineapples. The brakeman would toss the *Honolulu Advertiser* out for us. He had read it on the trip out around Kaena Point. On the way back to town later in the day, the men would toss large juicy pineapples to us kids as we frantically waved. We had been swimming, but when we heard the *hoo-hoo-hooie* of the coming train, we would rush out of the ocean, scramble up the sandy beach, and race around the tent to position ourselves on the railroad fence so we could hopefully catch the pineapples. That was the summer I got the most ghastly case of hives from eating so much pineapple.

We burned a lot of punk to keep the mosquitoes down. We ate a lot of barbecued chicken from live chickens we bought at Campbell's Mokuleia Ranch. Mother knew how to kill a chicken by slitting its throat. Being born and raised on a farm, she was farm-wise. She could make a little paper flame from a rolled-up newspaper and singe the dead chicken's feathers while I stood there admiring her dexterity and smelling the singed feathers. I at least learned how to make a decent fire in the barbecue, but I never had any desire to learn how to kill the chicken or pluck the feathers either. Mother thrust a paintbrush into my hand that summer and kept me very busy doing something besides swimming and eating pineapple. I was not a gracious worker, but I remember that I had no choice. When she was put out with me she would always say something like *"Betty Dyer, you come here and get busy."* Always both my names, as though they were one.

We had our meals outside sitting around the ping-pong table. When Mother built a barbecue fire, she always poured on a good half cup of kerosene before she tossed the match onto the heap of paper, kindling and charcoal. *Sa-woosh!* It would explode upwards. I copied her technique. Sometimes I just barely made it to safety as I jumped back when the fire exploded.

Naturally we had termites. In a single-wall house, damp from the ocean air, those termites were probably saying *"Yum yum, dinner's coming"* the minute the beams and siding were nailed together.

The day came when the walls and roof were finished. With great excitement the huge tent was carefully collapsed. Uncle Wilfred and Mr. Tanabe had to shove and grunt it through the 36 inch wide door.

"Ahhhh!" we all sighed with joy.

At last we could look out and see the ocean through our large sliding windows. The air moved freely in and out along all sides; the screens kept out the mosquitoes, and the outside shutters were let down and fastened when we locked up for the one-hour drive back to Waikiki.

If I were to recall the most often uttered words at Mokuleia they would be SHUT THE DOOR, and next would be DON'T *slam the door.*

We had huge cockroaches, enormous spiders, and once

Mokuleia Beach

in a while a creepy, crawly centipede, but it was still heavenly to be there.

Before we closed up the house we would literally hose down the floors and sweep the water out through the four-inch hole in the foundation that was thereafter plugged up again with a large wooden plug. My mother was inventive that way. We always walked into a clean house whenever we went to *the country*. All the dirt and the sand had been hosed out.

We would just throw open the shutters, open the windows for the ocean breeze, and shiver with joy at being there again.

Mother had furnished the house with auction-house furniture. She loved a bargain and she and her friend Betty Patterson, who later owned millions of dollars of Waikiki real estate, frequented the auction houses, since they both owned apartments and needed pieces of furniture from time to time. We inwardly groaned that Mother was furnishing our new house with old cast-offs.

One memorable day, the furniture arrived when the daily train arrived. We were standing in the empty beach house listening for the train whistle. When we heard it we ran to climb the fence along the tracks and wait. The engineer waved hello, and then the train came to a dead stop.

The next thing we knew, the engineer and the two brakemen were hoisting the beds, tables, chairs, and sofas over the six-foot rail fence and carrying everything right on into the house.

Presto chango! We were instantly furnished!

I'll bet I heard my mother tell her story of that day a hundred times, and I never got tired of it.

We ended up with a large high-ceilinged room about 22 feet by 28 feet with two small lean-to rooms on the sides. One was the kitchen and the other the bathroom. Originally, the toilet as well as the shower had an inside as well as an outside entrance. It was delightful to sit in the WC and have the outside door wide open so you could see the ocean and the sampans out at sea and the other kids walking on the reef.

All that changed later on when we added the bedroom next to the bathroom. Later on we also added what was known as *Mother's bedroom* and the tiny maid's room next to it. Mother's bedroom is still there, but the maid's room got wiped out when the house was partially demolished during the 1946 tidal wave.

Mother and Dad were on the mainland that April 1, 1946. No one was in the house when the ferocious waves hit. Later on they had the job of putting the house back together again.

The first wave struck Oahu at 7:00 A.M. The second wave was seven minutes later and the third wave a few minutes later. There was no warning. There had been a world-shaking undersea earthquake around 2:00 A.M. Hawaiian time about 2000 miles north of Hawaii in the Aleutian chain. The shakes continued for several hours. These triggered the tsunamis which hit the Hawaiian Islands a few hours later.

People who witnessed it said that the water drew back, and the entire reef that protects Crozier Drive from the seas was exposed down to the sand. The reef along that part of the beach consists of coral heads and other kinds of contiguous coral and is about a half mile wide and two

Mokuleia Beach

miles long. There were about sixty houses along Crozier Drive. When the water came back with a roar and a rush it lifted the surge clear up and over the tops of the houses along the shore.

Our front windows collapsed in a heap of glass and wood, and the furniture was slammed around and the beds were tossed here and there and the inside walls of the single-wall house shattered. Nothing was left standing except the back bearing wall, which helped to support the ceiling. It was a disheartening mess. It took weeks to clean up the debris and to shovel out the sand and to rebuild the house. For years afterward we picked up pieces of glass out in the yard.

All over the island of Oahu as well as the other islands, the damage was in the millions. Hilo on the Big Island was devastated.

Later on we got an eyewitness account of that memorable morning from a twenty-year-old neighbor girl, who instead of fleeing with her parents in their car, elected to stay. She climbed a tall coconut tree where she rode out the waves and observed the entire devastation first hand. We listened to her report with awe, shaking our heads at her courage.

Typically the way we were warned of an impending disaster in those days was for the army to send their men out to knock on our door and warn us of whatever it was they had heard was coming. We had other tidal wave alerts in subsequent years, and usually they came in the middle of the night. A loud pounding on the door and a man's voice shouting, "You have to get out; there's a tidal wave coming."

Born and Raised in Waikiki

Other waves did damage, but the wave of 1946 did the most.

During World War II and gas rationing, it was impossible to drive the sixty-four miles round trip out to Mokuleia and back to Waikiki, and since Mom and Dad figured my brother and I would probably live on the mainland, they decided to sell the beach house.

Jack and I were not consulted. It was done. They sold it for $6500.

The buyers turned out to be a black soldier and his wife. Later our irate neighbors told us that the buyers had had gambling in the house.

Mom and Dad had carried back the first deed of trust, and so when the buyers stopped making payments on the mortgage after the tidal wave, Mom and Dad legally took back the property two years later, on January 22, 1948.

We owned our beach house again, and I have always known that the Lord wanted us to have it back. The house was a total wreck, but we Dyers love nothing so much as a challenge. It was a joy to clean up the mess and to restore the house to something totally wonderful again.

The next time my mother thought about selling the house was in the 1960's. She put an ad in the paper inviting offers. I sat in the laundry tub with my long legs dangling over the side and my *okole* in the hot water soaking my painful hemorrhoids the day a potential buyer came to look. I leaned my head out and could see he was a handsome young Japanese man. I could hear Mother ask him to make an offer. Then I heard him ask Mother to name her price. She refused, and they had reached a standstill. She yelped for me to come and help her, and I recall shrieking

Mokuleia Beach

back to her, "*You got yourself into this! Get yourself out!*"

I continued to sit in the hot water, and the potential buyer left in disgust, and the subject of selling the house was never mentioned again.

I was destined to lose the house eventually. In 1973, I experienced the most emotionally painful event of my life. I gave up my half-ownership of the house.

Joint ownership was not working out comfortably. My only brother and his wife had the use of the house for ten months of the year, and we had it for two months every other year; but that was too often in their opinion. The only time we could be there was in the summer and that was the time they wanted it also. It did not appear that we could ever work it out to their satisfaction. We contributed to the upkeep, etc., and my husband made lots of improvements, but what they really wanted was to own it by themselves. It was hopeless.

After anguished discussion, I signed a quit-claim deed to the house and divided up the money I received, $25,000, by giving each of my five children five thousand dollars worth of General Motors stock and then tried to justify what I had done to them.

They were in shock, but they were also courageous kids and with tears in their eyes and in mine, we all locked up the house and walked away for the last time in August 1973.

When it came to really leaving that marvelous beach house for good I nearly died from the pain. I remember sitting on the beach with Katy, my brother's only daughter, and her asking me, "How do you feel?" and me replying, "I feel like someone cut off my arms and my legs."

Born and Raised in Waikiki

They used to send Katy to come and stay with us at Mokuleia, and she would brag that she was being raised *Eastern style*. Whatever the hell that was! Anyway my five kids more or less enjoyed her, and she livened up our dinner table. She taught us about Sallie Fish (selfish) and Jenny Ross (generous). She loved to sing and so did we, and so we learned to sing her crazy songs. One was,

"Jason, Jason, I've been thinking,
What in the world have you been drinking,?
Is it whisky, is it wine,?
OMIGOSH, it's TURPENTINE!"

The next year I went back to Honolulu all by myself, and with money I inherited from my parents, I bought a fee-simple condominium in a new project about two miles down the beach from the old beach house at the Mokuleia Beach Colony. It is all ours.

I remained on reasonably good terms with my only brother.

"Lead me not into temptation" became for me, the most meaningful part of the Lord's Prayer.

I prayed earnestly to resist the temptation to have a falling out.

CHAPTER 11

Dyer's Gift Shop

"I rushed to the store to tune the ukes and unpack the satin pillow cases..."

I really liked helping my father at our store at 1160 Fort Street. My friends would drop in to visit with my dad too. He liked them and they liked him. We were not allowed to park in front of the store; that space was for customers.

One could have walked up the Ewa side of Fort Street and shopped for clothes at Liberty House or McInerney's, bought a man's suit at The Hub and shopped for an expensive wedding present at Wichman's Jewelry Store. Further up the street, on the same side, one could buy fresh coconut candy and other delectables at Dye's Candy Shop or stop in at Wadsworth Photo to pick up one's prints.

If you were ready for lunch, the Blaisdell Hotel with hundreds of singing canaries welcomed you. Lunch could be a fresh fruit cocktail followed by a hot roast beef sandwich with mashed potatoes and gravy. Top it off with a chocolate sundae and wash it all down with iced tea—65 cents total.

After lunch one went next door to Dyer's Gift Shop. Across the lane was the next store, Watumull's East India

Born and Raised in Waikiki

Store—big competition for my dad's store. Watumull's expanded and went on to become a large chain of importers still in business as I write this. When my dad retired in 1943, Dyer's Gift Shop was sold to a jewelry and watch merchant and was no longer an Oriental import store.

On the Diamond Head side of Fort Street, one could buy shoes at McInerny's Shoe Store, shop at Andrade's Men's Store, order flowers at Fujikami's and then step in to Kress.

It caused a big stink when the mainland heads of Kress wanted to build on Fort Street in the thirties. Up until then, Honolulu had not had a mainland chain store. It was predicted to be the end of the small businessman. Nevertheless, Kress did come to Fort Street and it was a blessing because we had not had a real five-and-dime store.

On the corner of King and Fort Streets was E.O. Hall and Son. It was a hardware store and they also sold dishes. They suffered a fire in the thirties and everyone in Honolulu went to their *fire sale*. Mom dragged me along and I loved all the pushing and the frenzied buying. We bought our dishes for the beach house that day. Mom was in her glory buying bargains.

Across the street on the other corner was Benson Smith's Drug Store and if one wanted a hamburger one could climb onto the stool at the counter and order what they called a Juicy Jumbo. It might have been Parker Ranch beef with Maui onions grated into the beef. Simply delicious.

Dyer's Gift Shop cost $35.00 a day to operate. This included the rent to the Blaisdell Hotel and the salaries for Santiago and for Helen who worked in the store. Any income over $35.00 was all ours. Santiago was Filipino, and he pried open the crates that came from the Orient and

Dyer's Gift Shop

helped Daddy unpack the merchandise. Helen was Japanese nisei (second generation in Hawaii) and waited on the customers and strung and knotted the jade and the crystal beads. Daddy also offered that I could keep for myself every penny I earned selling antimony boxes. Today they sell for around $5.00, but back in the Thirties we sold them for thirty-five cents.

They were silver colored with raised relief carvings and lined with wood, about four by six inches, and were made in China. I wish you could have been there and walked into the wide glass front door of the store and seen me smile and get ready to lure you into buying one of the boxes. Daddy was observing my performance and getting a big kick out of my selling technique. I was equally happy to have such a challenge, and it was fun. I sold an awful lot of boxes. When I got years and years older I would sell a lot of real estate.

I would go down to the store on Saturdays and glue decals on koa wood boxes, napkins rings, and ukeleles. Dad bought the ukes wholesale from Mr. Kamaka himself of the famous Kamaka ukulele family. I knew how to tune the ukes, and when Franklin Roosevelt sent the fleet around the world in 1937 to show the world that the United States was strong and prepared, I tuned up dozens of ukes and strummed a few chords.

The fleet arrived one afternoon, anticipated but not announced. We knew the fleet was coming but we didn't know exactly when, and hundreds of us hurried to the beach after school and joined the hundreds more on the shore gazing out to the southern horizon.

The battleships *Mississippi* and *California* and *Tennessee* and *Arizona* and the carriers *Lexington* and *Saratoga* and their accompanying destroyers and cruisers finally came in view one by one, and the throng cheered wildly.

"THE FLEET'S IN!"

That night the United States fleet was anchored in a line offshore at Waikiki. Lights were strung from stem to stern on every ship and we all gathered on the beach ooohhing and aahing and getting goose bumps! It was the first exciting and positive thing that had happened in Honolulu in a long, long time.

I rushed to the store to tune the ukes and unpack the satin pillow cases that spelled *Mother or Aloha*, only $5.00 each. The cash registers were ringing again.

Those young men were all so clean and so happy to be on our exotic shores. Fort Street was a sea of white uniforms as they streamed up the sidewalks looking for souvenirs. They were looking for hula girls specifically, and girls generally. I was tall for my age and a born flirt, and I must have had a hundred chances to date, but I was too young, of course.

I can still smell the laundry soap and the starch from those white uniforms. And each man's cap was set at a different angle. They were all so young and laughed so much. I began to think I might be pretty, after all.

Before I leave off about Dyer's Gift Shop, there are a couple more things to remember. Fort Street for years had been one way going *DOWN*, and later in the Thirties after Honolulu acquired a city planner from the mainland, he decided that Fort Street from then on should be one way going *UP*.

On that momentous day of change, we all piled into our

Dyer's Gift Shop

cars and literally paraded *UP* Fort Street, gloriously honking horns and waving with wild abandon as though we were breaking the law.

CHAPTER 12

Opportunity Knocks

"The sun was hot on our skin but we were cool with our clothes off."

When I was in fifth grade at Punahou I won a dance try-out. I had a chance to get the part of the Queen in the spring pageant, but I had to *try-out* and, boy oh boy, I danced my heart out and got the part.

I hand-painted large flowers on a long skirt and a ruffled blouse Mom made from a white sheet. I wore a crown of flowers, and I was the center of attention and the prettiest girl there, and I still have the photograph to prove it. Well, anyway, I thought I was the prettiest. I have treasured that photograph all my life, a mute testimony to my young achievement. It made up for not being chosen to be a flower girl that earlier time in Seattle. I felt very good about this.

Punahou School gave me friends and memories to last a lifetime. Thank God my parents sent me there. It must have cost a lot, but they never complained. I heard over and over how they had *walked to church to save the nickel carfare* and I got the message. Economize.

I wanted to buy all my dresses at McInerny's instead of Liberty House. McInerny's could run nine to fourteen dol-

Opportunity Knocks

lars for a dress while Liberty House was a more modest five to seven dollars. We mostly shopped at Liberty House. The sales ladies all wore black in the winter and white in the hot months. My mother got all dressed up to take me shopping. Hat, gloves, the works! Liberty House, remember, was on the corner of Fort Street and King Street, just a couple of blocks down from my Dad's store. Mc Inerny's was further down Fort Street a couple blocks up from Aloha Tower where the boats docked. Fort Street was the main shopping street then, partly because of the many boats which docked nearby and the tourists who walked around while the boats were in port. Incidentally, we called them boats rather than ships. Saturday was Boat Day because that was the day the boat sailed for San Francisco. It would have sounded silly to call it Ship Day.

Sailors sailed on ships and tourists sailed on boats.

Honolulu was a stopover for the around-the-world cruises, and we got our share of titled people passing through: Lord and Lady So and So. The leading hostesses would vie for the honor of entertaining them. After all, Hawaii was noted for its hospitality.

I remember when Axel Wenner Gren, the Swedish munitions magnate, docked his yacht in Honolulu Harbor right by Aloha Tower. We went downtown to gawk at it. It looked big enough to be the *Lurline*, one of the popular Matson boats that sailed from the West Coast to Honolulu every week. The Swede was on his way to Japan and probably selling arms along the way. We laid out the red carpet for him too. It was a couple of years before World War Two began.

When I was twelve, I still didn't know where babies

came from, but about this time, Mom decided I needed to have a corset. She hauled me upstairs on Fort and Bethel Street to her corset lady.

This woman wore a lot of makeup and smelled of bath powder and cheap cologne. I hated being in her shop and exposing my body to her gaze. I got fitted with a monstrous pink contraption complete with stays and ties and long things hanging down on which to fasten stockings. It was supposed to be cinched up around my waist.

I heard Mom say to the corsetiere, "I don't know what I'm going to do with her; she's so tall." I died of embarrassment, as though being so tall was a serious defect. After the corset came home with me I strapped it on a couple of times and then I flung it way back in my closet and it was never mentioned again. But what Mom had said stayed in my head.

My cousin Billy De Jarlais, the son of Mother's brother, Wilfred, the one who helped to build the house on Crozier Drive, was living practically in our back yard in the little house his father had built when they came overfrom Seattle. Billy was a couple of years older than I, and he had an inkling what *it* was all about and a burning desire to try *it* out.

He and I would get in a rowboat over on the Ala Wai Canal. We'd paddle over to a quiet off-shoot of the main canal where there were tall grasses and then we'd take off our bathing suits and scooch way down in the boat.

No one could see us.

The sun was hot on our skin, but we were cool with our clothes off. We could see little white butterflies and hear the cars driving by, but they couldn't see us. We didn't

Opportunity Knocks

touch each other or do anything but lie there and feel mildly excited because we were naked.

One afternoon after checking to be sure my mother was away, we went from the canal straight upstairs to Uncle Wilfred's bedroom. Uncle Wilfred was downtown and Auntie Clara was with him, and so we had the place to ourselves. I knew something major was going to happen. Billy was very agitated. I could smell the Lifebuoy soap he always used. He had me lie down on his parent's bed and then he got on top and tried to insert himself. I was no longer having fun, and I wanted to get away but I soon realized nothing was going to happen anyway. Billy was frustrated or scared. I went home unscathed but shaken up.

I decided I'd better tell my Mother what had happened or hadn't happened. I think she almost died of shock and embarrassment. I was annoyed that I had been kept in ignorance all this time, and I knew my mother *had* to tell me the facts of life. *Now*.

We sat on the camphor chest in her room, and she explained what was supposed to happen between a man and a woman in order to create a new life. Her little explanation was pretty sketchy. She could have used one of those books they have now to explain everything. I vowed to myself that if I ever had children, I would keep them away from their cousins and I would tell them the facts of life at least by ten years of age.

I never saw Billy again, and Mother and I never spoke of the incident again.

By the time I got to junior high I was still very happy to be at Punahou and equally happy to be studying some interesting subjects, such as algebra and Latin and history.

We had grand teachers, Miss Porter, Miss Hasty, Miss Knudsen, all old maids and dedicated, wonderful teachers. I might have decided to become a teacher, but I was afraid if I did I'd be an old maid too.

We also had a vigorous athletic program, and even if I was not the star, I was pretty good. I participated in lots of after-school sports, and I won a silver medal twice. Not many girls won a silver, and only three or four won a gold medal. I hung them on my charm bracelet. One could earn points toward a medal by participating and I was determined to have a one. Two of my proudest moments were the two times my name was called to walk onstage and get the medals.

I was liked by the kids in my class, but I was taller than most of the boys, and I had very few dates. I might have been more popular with the boys if I had been more willing. I'll never know for sure.

But I do remember the evening Eddie Lloyd met me on Beach Walk. (May he rest in peace.) He lived on Lewers Road a block over, and we were both about thirteen, and he asked me to walk down to the beach with him.

It was getting after dark. The cannon at Fort De Russy had already gone off at sunset, and I was due home.

Something about the way he asked me made me uncomfortable and so I refused him. Eddie said, "Well, you know, opportunity only knocks once." I blushed and cringed all the way home. I think my instinct told me he wanted to neck or do something repulsive. I'd already had that experience! He never asked me out again.

About this time I told my folks that all my friends were

Opportunity Knocks

taking ballroom dancing classes. I wanted to go to that more than anything I had ever wanted. I pleaded and begged my dad but to no avail. I begged so bitterly and relentlessly that my dad finally flared and slapped my face—the only time he ever did that.

I probably accused them of never giving me anything. I held that against them for many years, because I always felt that I would have been better adjusted socially with the boys if I had had dancing classes with them.

Who knows what their reason was, but it certainly stunted my style for a long time. In fairness, they were probably afraid to let me out of their sight. Afraid of what might happen to me.

Afraid of another Cousin Billy.

CHAPTER 13

To the Orient

"By the time we got to the hotel, the first bombs had fallen."

The fourth big ocean voyage in my life was in 1937 when I was fifteen. I had been to the Northwest twice with my mother and to Ohio once with my father. Once again my dad surprised me by announcing out of the blue that we were going to go to the Orient together. I was thrilled. I had heard so much about the mysterious Orient from my mom and dad.

Dad went out there every September for at least six weeks. My brother had gone with him in 1933, and Mom had gone with him in 1927. Tokyo had had a huge earthquake in the early Twenties. The destruction was still evident.

This trip it was going to be my turn.

I rushed to the dressmaker and had some outfits whipped up. Mrs. Miura could copy any picture, and so I showed her clothes in fashion magazines and also made some sketches. One I was especially proud of was a pink sharkskin print. It had three pieces: a skirt with buttons covered with the same fabric, a short bolero jacket that buttoned at the waist, and a one-piece sleeveless play suit that

To the Orient

was the pits to get out of in order to go *shi, shi*. I could wear all three pieces at the same time as an outfit or I could wear them as separates. I wore it with saddle shoes and bobby socks and felt like a knockout rich tourist.

On board the ship was a famous composer. His name was Rudolf Friml and he was known as the composer of the "Indian Love Call" and other light opera songs. He took me to tea on the ship, just the two of us in the tea lounge, and best of all he flattered me by telling me I had the best-looking legs he had ever seen. Wow! I was finally getting some praise from a total stranger. And a glimpse of the possibilities that existed once I got older.

I was really terribly excited about the prospect of ten days on my favorite ship, the *Empress of Japan*. I felt as if I owned the ship because I had been on it before in 1931 and 1933 and knew my way around.

The ship had a huge ornately tiled swimming pool not located outside on deck as pools are now located but way down below deck. One could swim there in any kind of weather. It had beautiful dressing rooms and a massage room and a very high ceiling. It was a spectacular Esther Williams movie-star pool.

Ten days after sailing from Honolulu harbor, we were off the coast of Japan. We lined the ship's railing to catch our first glimpse of Mount Fuji. On the shore were rickshaws and endless bales of goods and crowds of people. Confusion everywhere. I was very excited and dying for a rickshaw ride, but that would come a day or so later.

We stayed at the Imperial Hotel in Tokyo. It had been designed by Frank Lloyd Wright and miraculously had survived the earthquake. Daddy's suppliers wanted to entertain us at dinners, and I was appalled by the slurping noises they made as they ate their food. I could hear their conversation saying that the enemy they most feared was not China but Russia. This all amazed me. They did not have bad table manners; they were showing their enjoyment of the meal when they made slurping noises. It was my first taste of what are now called cultural differences.

I visited Mr. Nakayama's place of business in Yokohama and felt very special. He arranged my visit to a dressmaker, where I pointed to a picture in *Vogue* magazine and selected some gold, silver, and pale-beige silk obi cloth in order to have an evening gown made.

It was a gorgeous dress, and I felt as if I were a princess in it. It traveled well and I was careful of it, and it had as much fun as I did. In fact it had another special outing in 1969 at the Inaugural Ball for Richard Nixon. It was by that time a vintage dress of thirty-five years. And in 1994, it came out of mothballs again when my daughter Stephanie wore it to Bill Clinton's Inaugural Ball. By that time the dress was fifty-six years old. When I had it pressed prior to loaning it to Stephanie, the presser told me it was the most beautiful dress she had ever seen and that it would "last a lot longer than we will."

Just to show you how naive I am, when we were planning our trip to Nixon's inaugural with our friends Russell Doe and Marilyn Doe, I actually fantasized about the president coming up at the ball and asking me to dance. Now I ask you, how dumb can a girl be! The Nixons were preceded into the Shoreham Hotel by the Marine band who immediately played ruffles and flourishes to announce the impending arrival of the president. After a short greeting

To the Orient

and a big wave, the Nixons hurried on to their next ball. That was it!

I was fascinated by the geishas in Tokyo. We walked into their district one evening as they were preparing to go to their various entertainment houses. Each girl was having her makeup applied: very white powder on her face and neck and the back of her neck and the upper part of her back, her make-up applied on her face and her black hair arranged in an elaborate headdress high on her head. Later a beautiful kimono and *tabis* (socks) and *geta* (slippers) would complete her costume. All of the geishas were strikingly beautiful.

We also went to the Takarazuka Opera. It was a musical light opera type of entertainment including a chorus line. This particular night I was astonished to hear them singing a popular American song "In the Chapel in the Moonlight," singing it totally in Japanese, of course.

We visited some friends in Kobe. He was the Swedish consul, Mr. Pearce, and his wife was Eurasian. Because of her Japanese blood, they were not fully accepted in society. There were even certain mountain resorts where they were not welcome. I heard all this by eavesdropping on my parents' conversations. I thought they were charming people, but there was an underlying sadness. They had a daughter, and she suffered the same discrimination.

Outside of Tokyo is a little seaside resort. Daddy had friends there too. I took my bathing suit with me and I had a dip in the sea followed by my first and last Japanese-style bath. I was instructed by the lady of the house how to pour water over myself and then soap up and then rinse again using the dipper provided and finally how to immerse myself in the wooden tub of hot water. I didn't think much of the complicated Japanese style of taking a bath after that experience.

We also went to Miyanoshita and visited the waterfall and then to Lake Hakone to hopefully get a view of Mount Fuji, called Fuji-san. It was just as beautiful as the many pictures we had seen of it. We also spent the night at Nara in a genuine Japanese inn, slept on tatami mats, and heard the creek as it fell across the pebbled creek bed. We wore kimonos (not a unique experience for this little Hawaiian kid) and we saw the beautiful red lacquer temples and heard the huge temple gongs. It was all very exotic, and I was enthralled by it.

We took another ship, the *President Hoover*, to Kobe and then to Hong Kong, Shanghai, and eventually to Manila. Hong Kong was the most glamorous city I had ever seen. As I stood on deck while the ship was being tied up I could see dozens of tall, handsome Englishmen dressed in white uniforms with the customary tropical look: long shorts, knee-length socks with little tassels, white shoes and white sun helmets on their heads. I was smitten with all of them.

Since the ship was docked on the Kowloon side, we had to ride the ferries day and night in order to get on the island of Hong Kong. Such smells and such crowds of people, and for the first time I saw families living on the flat boats of the river. Life went on day by day, and they seldom left the boats they were born on. Huge mounds of rubbish as well as huge mounds of merchandise were transported by these boats.

The ferries were incredibly crowded in the daytime, and fortunately it was a short ride. You could see the city of

To the Orient

Hong Kong rising from the harbor clear up to Victoria Peak.

By far the most glamorous thing that had ever happened to me occurred when Daddy steered me into a *hole-in-the-wall* jewelry shop. There I was introduced to Mr. Wu, the owner of the shop. Daddy bought unset semiprecious stones from him for our store. Mr. Wu was expecting us, and he was prepared to dazzle a young fifteen-year-old girl. He opened his large safe very deliberately and from it he withdrew a packet that would fit into a shoe box. After laying out a black velvet cloth, he opened the packet and emptied out the contents: diamonds, rubies, emeralds, star sapphires, aquamarines. I could hardly believe my eyes. I felt as if I were a part of Arabian Nights.

Daddy picked out several stones, and then I was given a choice of the blue zircons. I picked out earrings, a bracelet, and one deep-blue stone which was made into a ring later on. As we left that shop I was in a daze of delight.

It was 1937 and the war had not begun. People were everywhere going about their business dressed in long coolie pants and jackets. Laundry was hanging out to dry on bamboo poles from seemingly every window as we picked our way along the sidewalk, trying not to step on beggars or in dirty puddles.

Later on we drove around to the other side of the island to Repulse Bay, and I went swimming in the dark-green water. Still later that afternoon we went to the world famous Peninsula Hotel for tea, and I got a glimpse of what it was like to be a Caucasian man or woman in this jeweled city of the Orient. There were beautifully-gowned women wearing their strands of pearls and handsome men in their white linen suits sipping tea or alcoholic concoctions and eating little cakes and looking as though they hadn't a care in the world.

The ship was in port for two full days, and so the second day we trained to Canton, where we wormed our way down narrow and smelly alleys and through several low-stooped gateways, and eventually ducked down into a low-ceilinged workroom where the most gorgeous robes were being embroidered. When our eyes had grown accustomed to the light, we could see a half dozen women dressed in black coolie jackets and hunched over their embroidery work. The scene was happy but intense. The women were chattering in Chinese, and they looked up and smiled at us. I was amazed at what I saw.

Spread out on a large flat table surface were colorful Mandarin coats: white, red, black, and jade green. The coats were in the traditional style: very full, long sleeves, high Mandarin collars, midcalf length, and very full around the body. The women were adding the gorgeous and colorful embroidery that makes these coats unique and so expensive. The women continued their work as we visited with the head lady. Basically Daddy was there to show me around and to order some coats for his store. As I recall we sold them for $200 apiece in Dyer's Gift Shop.

From Hong Kong, we went to Shanghai. This time we were in a hotel, the Park Hotel, and it overlooked the park, which was also the racetrack. It was arranged differently from any hotel I had previously known in that the entry was a very small foyer with an elevator entrance and attendant. The front desk and the lobby-cocktail lounge were on the next floor above.

To the Orient

This was the first week of August 1937. By the 10th of August, China would never be the same. Japan, who had already invaded Manchuria, had decided to continue her plan of aggression into China.

I was invited to a birthday party for the daughter of some of Dad's American friends. They lived in what was called the International Settlement. Theirs was a very large house with porches and waving fans and lots of fresh air and sunshine and servants in white coolie dress, which was white pants and white jackets with frog closings, and padded slippers on their feet. There seemed to be many servants and dozens of houses in this walled settlement.

They took us to a place that was a favorite of Americans in Shanghai. It was called The Chocolate Shop. We had hot dogs and milk shakes there. Not exactly like the ones from Benson-Smith's on Fort and King Street, but a welcome change from hotel and ship fare, and definitely more to my liking than the food the night before.

After lunch we went to the movies to see an American film. It was an Edward G. Robinson gangster movie. I was surprised that we were almost the only people in the movie house. It looked like a command performance. I was further surprised to see my father sitting in another row in the theater.

After the movie was over we trooped out onto the sidewalk and immediately were aware that something fearful was happening. People were rushing in all directions. Even the beggars were not to be seen in their usual places on the sidewalk. Cars were blaring their horns as they sped past. Obviously something had happened or was about to happen and I was thankful that my Daddy was there to help me get back to the hotel.

By the time we got to the hotel, the first bombs had fallen and there was complete pandemonium. People were scared, and that included me. Obviously people had been killed but we didn't know how many.

I said to the elevator man something like, "Oh, it's *terrible* to think about people getting killed!"

"Oh, we got plenty more Chinese people," he answered.

I was shocked at this callous lack of sensitivity. Another lesson learned.

We knew there were dozens of foreign correspondents fresh from the war in Spain staying at the Park Hotel. They had their typewriters and their binoculars and every so often they would leave their spot in the lounge and go up on the roof-top and observe the war activity approximately fifteen miles from the city in a district called Chai Pei.

They would come back down off the roof and sit at their tables again, clap their hands and yell *Boy*, and a white-coated waiter would bring them their beer, gin, or whatever and then they would write their dispatches.

Being fifteen years old, I was old enough to see that they had not endangered their lives any more than I had, and yet they were able to write and get paid for writing and could send off their stuff to be read as the truth by millions of readers all over the world. I knew a lot of it was educated guess work.

A skeptic was born!

The day the bombs fell was August 10, 1937, and thereafter was called Bloody Saturday. Before we left Shanghai as refugees a few days later, I had seen a shocking reality of war. It was a truck loaded with dismembered bodies.

To the Orient

There were bloodied torn-off legs piled on top of arms and part torsos of bodies with the insides visible and sometimes the heads half torn off. They looked as if they had been shoveled into the truck without regard for the humanity of the victims. No one had bothered to cover the carnage from view. All individuality had been merged into blood and gore. The sight was unforgettable.

We were now officially refugees.

Instead of taking the train to Peking as planned, we had to get the heck out of there as fast as possible. Dad was able to book two cabins on the *President Hoover*. Mine was room thirteen on the top/boat deck. Dad's was elsewhere. We left Shanghai the next evening on a riverboat that was to transport us down river to the mouth of the Yangtze River where the *Hoover* was sitting on the mud waiting for us and the tide.

We were anxious as we sat on the benches on the riverboat by the Bund, waiting for the coolies to load the baggage and the other passengers to get aboard. We all feared another air attack. We were a mixture of tourists and many missionaries.

The missionary families were a very frightened group. They had had to leave hurriedly and take only a few things with them. They had been living in China, some of them, for most of their lives. The little ones clung to their parents, and it was easy to read fear and confusion in their faces. I felt so sorry for them and so unable to really do anything to help. Their whole lives had been disrupted and probably changed forever.

After a long, anxious wait, the riverboat started up and we chugged and drifted down the Yangtze to where our ship lay in waiting. We boarded, had some tea, and looked over our rooms and then wandered up to the main promenade deck.

To my disbelief we could see on the shore not more than a mile away troops wearing camouflage outfits, carrying rifles, and occasionally shooting at something in the distance. Some of the soldiers had little branches tied to their helmets. I felt like I was watching a movie being filmed, but it was real life and the soldiers were part of the Chinese Army.

I decided to write my mother a note and tell her of our experiences in Shanghai. I was seated at a desk in the writing room scribbling away when I heard airplanes flying over. They sounded as if they were diving over us, and the next thing I knew I heard the whistle of a falling bomb and then the horrendous explosion of the bomb hitting the ship.

Everything shuddered! Glass was shattering everywhere, mirrors crashing and breaking and the ship's sirens were wailing and where, oh, where was my daddy? Common sense told me to get as far down in the ship as I could in case more bombs were coming. So I rushed down a wide stair-case, avoiding the crashing glass and the shards, ran past the purser's office and people milling around and down two more stairways, and finally after running through the dining room and through the huge galley, I found the ladder to the engine room. I stopped and looked around.

There were other passengers standing there, and then the most incredible thing happened. I looked at each of the perhaps a dozen men and women and children standing

To the Orient

there with me and one of the kids about my age looked very familiar, so familiar, in fact, that I recognized him as a Punahou classmate from first grade.

"Reggie Abbey, what are *you* doing here?"

About then my father showed up looking very pale and very relieved to find me unharmed.

We congregated in the dining room and spent several more rumor-filled hours waiting for the tide to come in and we had enough water under the ship so that we could float and leave. Those of us able to eat were given some crackers and ginger ale. I begged my father for a cup of coffee. It looked so reassuring, but he said I was still too young.

My cabin had been damaged by the bombs, and I was given another cabin. The bombs were actually dropped by the Chinese because they thought we were a Japanese troop ship. I think in a small way I learned another lesson about the inaccuracies of war.

Being passengers on the *President Hoover* meant that we had to go where it was going, and that meant to Manila and then Hong Kong again and finally to Yokohama and at last home to Honolulu.

When we were in Manila, we went to see the house and bedroomwhere General Aguinaldo, a Filipino hero, had been assassinated, and afterward we went to a cockfight. There were bleachers set up in a kind of barn and the place was filled with frantic Filipinos standing up and cheering wildly for the fighting cock they had bet on. The cocks were brilliantly colored, but with the knives fastened to their feet they were trained to be vicious and to kill their opponents

Born and Raised in Waikiki

I thought both tourist attractions were disgusting.

We got back to Honolulu in time for my junior year at Punahou. I had acquired a beautiful evening gown, a lot of lurid memories, and some healthy skepticism.

I was definitely growing up.

CHAPTER 14

Jack and Mabel

"She donned an amazing array of old clothes and a bathing cap on her head. I prayed none of my friends would see me with her."

We were all in awe of my father. With his Irish temper, he could blow up over the least little thing. He did not cuss, but he could glower something fierce. He just liked to have everything run smoothly and silently, if possible. He never went out and played poker, he didn't stop and have a drink with the boys. He worked very hard in his store. He loved to travel and he liked to tell funny stories, but at the dinner table we were all pretty subdued. You might say he *ruled the roost*.

We frequently had tourists for dinner during the winter months. Daddy would meet them at his store and befriend them and invite them to dinner. I think he was hungry for mainland conversation. Mother didn't seem to mind. Pop would tell his stories and Mom would tell hers.

Mom's story was about the salesman from the mainland who went into a local office and asked to see the boss. He was told in pidgin English, "Boss no stop." He sat down to await the boss's return. After a very long wait, he decided to ask another question, "When boss come back?" "Boss? Oh, boss, he go Japan." Mom would laugh and laugh over this story.

Pop's stories were usually about the Orient. My personal favorite was the one about the time he was on a steamer going up the Yangtze River. It was an overnight trip, and when it came time to go to sleep he turned out the overhead light. His cabinmate turned it back on. Pop got out of bed and turned it back off. The Chinaman turned it back on. This went on several times without any talk between them.

Finally, Pop got out of bed for one last time, unscrewed the bulb and *tossed it out the porthole.*

The night Franklin D. Roosevelt was elected in 1932, Dad and I were in the audience at the Pawaa Theater and when it was announced that Roosevelt had won, people started to sing "Happy Days are Here Again." I sang like crazy but I didn't know what for!

Soon after, when the Depression really hit, I remember my Daddy saying at the dinner table that from now on we had to pay more Income Tax. He was outraged! He switched his registration and never voted for a Democrat again as long as he lived.

My Dad died in June of 1960, and so I never found out if he would have voted for Kennedy, a Democrat, also a Catholic.

I remember overhearing that so and so made $10,000 a year. That was BIG MONEY in the Thirties. I don't know if Dyer's Gift Shop ever did that much. But with the income from the apartments added to the income from the store it was enough to send my brother to Harvard and Harvard Law School and me to Mt. Holyoke and Stanford.

Mom, my brother, and the dog and I always breathed a

Jack and Mabel

sigh of relief when Dad would leave for his annual six weeks buying trip to the Orient. While Dad was away, we ate out every night, played a lot of wee golf, and had fun. We even laughed at the dinner table.

Thanks to Mabel Dyer's prodding, I have good posture. I wish I had a nickel for every time my Mother poked me between the shoulder blades and told me, "Stand up straight, Betty Dyer."

How I hated to be poked that way. To this day I don't like anyone to touch me unless invited.

I resisted my mother as much as possible. I felt somewhat superior to her. Probably because we were not the same physical size (she was only 5'5") and our childhoods were so different. I think if my Mother had been more open with me about her life before she married I could have felt some empathy. She was a terrible tease. I always felt as if I was sparring with her.

However, in fairness, it is with thanks to my Mother that I developed what talent I had. She was the one who sent me off for piano lessons and ukelele lessons, and she was the one who goaded me into painting my first picture in 1955.

It was in the Fifties, and we were all staying on Crozier Drive at Mokuleia that summer. One day Mom urged me and kept urging and I kept protesting that I didn't know how to paint, and she kept saying "How do you know until you try?" and I finally gave in.

I bought some water colors and a pad and some brushes and headed up to her favorite view. It was Kolekole Pass on the Pineapple Road on Oahu.

I remember I parked the car way off the road and found

just the right view and dipped my brush into the water and then into the paint and then onto the paper. It felt terrific. I could see the results right away. My brain connected with my heart and my mind and I discovered I loved the feeling of creating something original.

No one was looking over my shoulder telling me what to do and how to do it. I splashed away happily, swatting pineapple bugs and noticing shapes and colors I had never seen before. It was exhilarating. And my Mother had been the one who got me started.

When I got home that day, I felt like a new woman. And the picture I had created turned out to have some vigor and some authenticity. I don't think I ever thanked her for getting me started. I didn't really believe I was good, but I knew I had a flair and that I enjoyed the whole process.

After that day I spent hours at night cranking out more and more scenes from my memory and imagination. Eventually I studied art at the local college and tried seriously to perfect whatever talent I had.

When I was a teenager, Mom had taught me to sew. She also enrolled me in sewing classes, and since she did not find fault with my work I really enjoyed sewing with her.

My father never once complained about my being tall like my mother did. He instilled in me the idea that I could do anything. He really wanted me to be a show girl. He kept encouraging me to have three skills; singing, dancing and playing an instrument. His pride in me was embarrassing at times.

After I was out of college and living on Beach Walk again in 1944 and dating young officers during wartime, my father would wait up for me in his white nightshirt in

Jack and Mabel

order to bid me good night. One night he came out onto the porch, where I am sure I was locked in the arms of the current flame and was unaware of his presence until he blurted out, "Time to come in, Bet."

The next morning all hell broke loose, and I hit the ceiling and covered all the bases of my age and stage in life, and he never embarrassed me again.

Another night I was all dressed to go out, and I had on a very pretty red dress. Daddy amazed me by saying that I should wear something else because in his words *nice girls don't wear red.*

When I wrote home from Mount Holyoke at the end of my freshman year, 1940, I told my Dad that I was now smoking cigarettes, and I didn't want to smoke behind his back.

I also told Dad that I needed a few bucks in order to get back to Honolulu for summer vacation, and as an aside, I asked him the name of our new maid.

Dad wrote back that he didn't want me to smoke, but if I did he would honor my wishes. He sent me $100. And he wrote that the new maid's name was *BETTY*.

In the later 1930's Mom bought a lot for $16,000 on Pacific Heights, where it was lovely and cool. She wanted to move out of Waikiki, where it was beginning to get crowded. Even though we would drive up there often and sit in the car or walk over the property, something kept her from building up there. It was at the top with a gorgeous view of Honolulu and clear out past Pearl Harbor to the Waianae mountains. They probably did not have the ready cash to build. They had survived the Depression and were putting my brother through college, and I would be next.

Born and Raised in Waikiki

That meant besides tuition and room and board, lots of train and ship transportation to get there.

When Jack graduated from Harvard he did not want any of us there. Mom and Dad were looking forward to being there because Jack was the first one in our family to graduate from college. My parents had traveled all over the world and were definitely not *hayseeds* but Jack still didn't want them there to see him graduate. They were bitterly disappointed.

Mom had started building apartments in Waikiki in 1926, and we had three apartments on Saratoga Road, all in one nice building, in addition to the two small apartments next to the garage in our back yard. So we had extra income all the time.

I helped her as little as possible. She used to say to me, "I hope your kids do you the way you do me!"

None of my friend's mothers had to work with rentals the way my mom did. If need be, my mother would clean the apartments if Masa could not, and then Mom would wash the slipcovers and put them back on the furniture. My mother was working her hardest to supplement the store's income so that my brother and I could have the college education she had not been able to have.

My brother and I had been little or no help to our mother in her work to manage these rentals. My regular Saturday job was to sweep out the carports at the apartments on Saratoga Road. The huge monkey pod tree Mom planted is still there. Once in a while when I was older, I would sit in a vacant apartment and show it to prospective tenants, and if I rented it Mom would give me five dollars. Mom would offer to give the tenant the 12th month free if they

Jack and Mabel

stayed a year. It was still the Depression.

Later on, in 1937, Mom had the two-story apartment building, designed by Roy Kelley, built on Kuhio Avenue. Furnished with rattan, the apartments were really lovely. The breeze blew through them, and they rented easily, $65.00 a month.

Mom and Dad were amazingly trusting with letting me use the car. I was a good driver, and Mom had taught me to drive with my head and not with the brakes. One time the car was parked in our driveway, and I forgot to put the gear-shift in neutral, and when I pressed on the starter, the Buick *shot forward* and crashed into the garage door. Not too much damage, fortunately, but I can still see and hear my Mother shouting out our back door, **"Betty Dyer, WHAT IN THE HELL ARE YOU DOING?!"**

Mother had a Ford coupe, a two-door car. Really quite *sporty*. It cost $500 new, and eventually, when it needed a paint job, my very own mother decided she could tackle it.

She donned an amazing array of old clothes and wore a bathing cap on her head. What a sight. She backed the car out of the garage and away from the house in case the paint sprayer got out of hand. I prayed none of my friends would see me with her.

She had a spray nozzle attachment on the vacuum cleaner, and she thinned the paint to the desired consistency, papered the windows and started to spray. Somewhere in the process some sand got on the car, not a whole lot, but enough to mar the effect. The car ended up a ghastly beige with flecks of sand.

Mom was not defensive about her completed job. She just did not want to discuss it.

Born and Raised in Waikiki

During the Depression Mom also used other money saving devices. For instance, she dry-cleaned our clothes.

She bought a small container made out of light-weight steel, and I would say it looked like a waste-basket with a handle. The clothes were swished around by the action of the handle turning the basket inside the container. For cleaning fluid Mom bought some naphthalene.

It stunk to high heaven, and when we went to church wearing the clothes she had cleaned, you could smell us coming down the aisle.

In 1938, Mom and her friend she'd met on her honeymoon, Clara Ludders, made plans to travel around the world. Clara had made some profits in small real estate ventures in Waikiki that my Mom had encouraged her to buy, and so the two ladies bought their travelers checks and made their plans. Their friends jealously predicted that they would not be friends by the end of their trip. They had an hilariously good time and we never tired of hearing their funny stories, especially the one about them being hauled up the side and into the ship in the cargo net because they had gotten back to the dock in Yokohama too late to walk up the gangplank. Clara's shoe fell off on the way up, and everyone watching cheered! This story seems to provide the mood of the whole trip.

Clara's husband, Hugo, had been born in Germany, and so they planned to visit Hugo's sisters in Bremen. They went to hear Hitler speak in the stadium. When the two ladies got back to Honolulu, Clara retold many times of how impressed she was with Hitler.

After the war started in 1939, Mother was told by one of Clara's friends that Clara had better pipe down, and that

Jack and Mabel

people were saying Clara was pro-Nazi.

A few months after the United States declared war on Japan and Germany after the Pearl Harbor attack on December 7, 1941, Clara and her husband Hugo were placed under arrest and interned on Sand Island in Honolulu Harbor. It was a terrible blow to their pride. Their indiscretions did not include being actual traitors, and when their trial finally took place after several months in detention, my mother had the courage to appear before the Military Tribunal to vouch for their loyalty. Clara and Hugo were subsequently allowed to go home.

Clara recovered her equanimity. She referred to being in jail, and regaled us with horror stories as well as stories of being the cook for all the inmates. The horror stories involved threats of rape by the guards.

Afterward, when we would be with Clara and Hugo at the beach house, Clara would make the most wonderful coffee cake in huge pans. She'd always say jokingly, "I learned to cook like that when I was in jail."

Hugo would wince when she said it. It never stopped being hurtful for him.

Mother was wearing herself out keeping the apartments rented and cleaned and I was not much help, and so she hired a succession of young Japanese girls to be maids. They got their room and board and fifteen dollars a week. They usually faded fast.

Mother brought one young Japanese girl in from Waialua, and the plan was that she would be trained in our house and learn the ways of housekeeping in a *haole* (Caucasian) home. She was amazingly literal and deep dumb.

I remember once we had company from Chicago and

were having a dinner party, and Mother asked her to serve the coffee with the dessert, and when the dessert arrived the maid had poured the coffee over it.

Eventually Mom found what she needed to convince herself this one really had to go. She discovered a whole pile of fifty-cent pieces on the back porch where the girl slept. Questioning revealed that the girl had been doing a thriving business with the soldiers from nearby Fort De Russy, and she charged fifty cents for each trick. Mom was horrified. She sheepishly drove the poor kid back to her house in Waialua.

I have driven by that little plantation house many times since then and always wondered what happened to Yuri-san.

Once when we needed a new maid, Dad told Mom that he would do the interviewing.

A series of prospective young Japanese girls stopped by the store in order to apply for the job.

Finally, after listening to their demands, Pop had had it and he told the last applicant the following.

"You can stay in bed as late as you like in the morning. Mrs. Dyer will bring you your breakfast in bed. You can have every afternoon off, and Betty will do the dishes at night."

Pop came home fairly bursting with this story because the poor girl had believed him!

He was choking with laughter and could hardly get the story out.

One of the maids played the Sami-sen, and most evenings she could be heard loudly whining her Japanese songs and accompanying herself on the stringed instrument.

Jack and Mabel

I don't recall her name, but she was the one who taught me the Japanese song I have used for fun ever since. It is actually a child's song and is called "Moshi Moshi Kame-san" ("Hello, Mr. Tortoise"). Put me in the vicinity of a group of Japanese people, and I will burst into this song to the amazement and amusement of all.

For example, one rainy night my husband Jim and I were enclosed inside the Waialua taxi along with five other passengers. We were going from the inter-island airport out to Mokuleia.

One of the passengers was the distinguished editor of the Japanese language newspaper, another was a young Japanese man from a Waialua plantation family, vacationing from Harvard and on his way to visit his parents. Two others were unidentified young Japanese girls who giggled all the time.

Anyway, it was pouring rain, the windows were fogged over with our breathing, and nothing had broken the ice. So I nudged Jim (we were in the front seat with the driver) and I started to sing my Japanese song.

"Moshi-moshi, kame-san, kame-san yo,
Seikai no uchi de omae hodo,
Ayumi no noroi mono wa nai,
Doshite son nani noroi noka."

It was such a marvelous shock to all our car-mates that they joyfully joined in, including the editor, and we rocked all the way out to Waialua.

Another time I was alone in my house in Visalia, and already in for the night when the phone rang and my friend Kay Harrell called.

"What are you doing?"

Born and Raised in Waikiki

"I'm in bed."

"Well, get your clothes on and come over and help us entertain a busload of Japanese businessmen we invited to visit us tonight."

So I threw on a muumuu and grabbed my uke and wondered, what next? Standing around the Harrell's kitchen sipping wine were at least twenty sweaty businessmen trying to make conversation with a very difficult language barrier.

At some point I decided that this was getting boring, and so I started to play the uke and sing, "Moshi-Moshi Kame-san."

The men burst into the song and dance, and the evening ended up with most of them sitting in Kay and Bob's hot tub having a memorable if slightly wacky American experience.

My daughter Sally learned the song, and so the tradition will not die.

CHAPTER 15

My Faith

"I still call myself a Catholic, but I can worship God with anyone."

St. Augustine's Catholic church is on Kalakaua Avenue across from the beach and one block from the Honolulu Zoo. You could walk out the front of church and see if the surf was up.

Movie stars went to Mass there, stars such as Irene Dunne and Loretta Young and Robert Young and his family. We always wondered how much they put in the collection, and it was difficult not to stare at them. The church was not air-conditioned back then. It had wooden latticework on three sides, and the breeze blew in from the ocean, and the little sparrows flew in and perched on the overhead beams.

As for going to church, it was never a question of *if*. It was more a question of *when*. We went every Sunday. We usually sat in the same pew, up near the front on the left side, and we gave money regularly and generously. Eventually the church came up with the idea of everyone giving their donation in a marked envelope, but my Dad never used the envelopes. One time we went to the Catholic church in Seattle, and the ushers collected our donation on the way in. My mother was incensed. She bristled that "they are making us pay to get in."

Daddy thought the sermons at St Augustine's were pretty awful, because back then Hawaii had missionary priests from Belgium, and their spoken English was difficult to understand. He longed for good sermons such as he had heard growing up on the mainland, sermons by an intellectual Jesuit or a hellfire-and-damnation Redemptorist.

I respected my mother's deep but non-demonstrative faith. I never saw her saying the rosary and she didn't attend Novenas, but I felt without a doubt her faith was satisfying to her. It was not unusual to see her make the sign of the cross. In itself, it is a prayer. *I believe in the Father, the Son, and the Holy Spirit.*

Dad was set in his ways and said his night time prayers kneeling down in the living room. We didn't pray with him. This was his own particular ritual, and he followed it regardless of who else might be in the room at the time. If he was on his way to bed, he knelt down and said his prayers. They took about three minutes. It is my most lasting impression of my father.

While I was in high school, I had what was almost a religious experience. Two priests of the Redemptorist Order came to St. Augustine's parish to conduct a mission. It went on for a week with lectures every evening. My Mother dragged me along with her. I wasn't eager but not objecting either. I was curious. They were fabulous speakers, men of conviction in their delivery. They preached the presence of the Holy Spirit and of grace. At the conclusion of the mission one of them said as though to me personally, "From now on, you will be filled with grace and the

My Faith

Holy Spirit will be with you forever."

I believed that to be the way it was and the way it would always be.

When it came time for me to be confirmed, I was one of about a half dozen Punahou kids who were allowed to leave school early so we could go across the street to St. Patrick's Church, where I was given confirmation instructions by a very fat and cranky Maryknoll sister. She did not impress me.

I knew I was going to receive the sacrament of Confirmation, but the one I really was looking forward to was the sacrament of Marriage. I had already received Baptism, Penance (confession), and Holy Eucharist (Communion), and I sure as heck wasn't interested in Holy Orders (religious life).

So my religious life was nurtured by my parents. They set the example, and I willingly followed it. Even all-night bull sessions at college could not shake my faith.

I believed that God made the world, that He made me, and that I was supposed to love my neighbor as myself, and that I was supposed to love Him and serve Him in this world so that I would be happy with Him in the next.

At that time the Catholic Church was a lot more rigid than it is today. For instance, I was not supposed to go to another church or be a bridesmaid in a wedding at another church. When my brother came home from Boston and reported how liberal the priests were there, it was an eye-opener for us.

We had a circle of friends who were decidedly cosmopolitan and broad-minded. I don't think we had any friends in Honolulu who actually went to our church. It

Born and Raised in Waikiki

came as an ugly surprise later in life to find out that there was prejudice against me because I went to the Catholic Church.

All through my years at college I attended church regularly. At Mount Holyoke College I even had to tramp through the snow to get there. Occasionally, after I got to Stanford, I got a ride to Mass with another junior transfer named Eunice Kennedy who had a brother named Jack. Then along came the Ecumenical Conference, and everything changed.

I maintained this strict observation of my faith until I was through raising children, but by the time I was in my middle fifties, the Mass was very different from what I had always loved. No longer were the beautiful introduction-to-the-Mass prayers said, or the prayers over the water and wine intoned in English or Latin so that the congregation could hear them.

> *"I will go in unto the altar of God, to God who gives joy to my youth. Our help is in the name of the Lord who made Heaven and earth."*

> *"Oh God who in creating human nature didst wonderfully dignify it and still more wonderfully has renewed it, grant by the mystery of this water and wine that we may be made partakers of thy divinity who didst vouchsafe to become partaker of our humanity."*

The mass was being invaded by people who played guitars and sang atrociously banal songs in an impossible key. And they expected the congregation to sing along with

My Faith

them. All the old standard hymns were relegated to the dumpster. I have not sung *"Holy God We Praise Thy Name"* in years, but I could belt it out if only I had a chance.

Gone was the glorious Easter music, gone was the fasting before communion from midnight the night before, gone were the head coverings. It was all so very different.

I didn't adjust easily. I kept trying, and sometimes I felt at home, but often I wondered what church I was in and why was I there. I went to a Mass at Georgetown University and heard the priest say, "Don't come to me to confess your sins. Go tell the person you sinned against that you are sorry."

I began to question the authority of the Church. I knew I believed in divorce under some circumstances, such as abuse and gross infidelity. I had heard about couples who were married over twenty years and had children and then were granted a church annullment and were able to marry someone else.

There seemed to be a double standard, and I asked myself why. I was adamant in my conviction that priests should be allowed to marry if that was their need. I do not believe that celibacy should be imposed.

As for birth control, I knew I had practiced birth control for years, and that most of the people who went to church with me were also practicing some form of birth control. As for abortion, I have very mixed feelings. I can understand the need in some cases, but I fear it is a sin. I blame men for not taking more responsibility and protecting the woman. But I blame the Catholic Church even more for not coming out in favor of birth control. I'd like to call it conception prevention.

Born and Raised in Waikiki

Years ago a dear friend told me this little joke.

"Say, Betty, do you know what they call people who use the rhythm method of birth control?"

"No, what?"

"PARENTS!"

I won't try to explain the rhythm method, the Catholic Church's so called *natural method* of birth control. Get a priest to 'splain it to you.

Despite my gripes, I kept up my prayer life. My father had shown me the way by his example. I still call myself a Catholic but I can worship God with anyone. One of my most recent adventures in faith was a visit to the Beale Street Baptist Church in Memphis, Tennessee. That place throbbed with joyous praise to the goodness of the Lord.

My mother and father's faith was more private than public, but it rubbed off on me, and I have made my choice to hold fast.

I will fight the good fight and keep the faith.

"I have loved, O Lord, the beauty of thy house and the place where thy glory dwelleth. Take not away my soul with men of blood."

My First Holy Communion picture in 1930

Christmas party, 1929. Helen Duryea, Marney Bellows, Marian Isenberg, Frances Dower, Peggy Kellerman, Pat Smith, two girls whom my mother invited much to my disgust, "Meskie McCuaig" and me, next to the tree

Haleiwa Beach on a trip around the island in 1926

My dog Kam and me about 1933

*My brother Jack and my dad on the ship
about to sail for Japan, in 1935*

Mr. Nakayama of Yokohama and my dad in 1937

My dad on a camel at the Great Wall of China

On Orient Visit

THREE MONTHS — Miss Betty Dyer, who with her father, John Dyer, left last week on the Empress of Japan for three months' tour of the Orient. They plan to visit Japan and China. Dyer is the owner of Dyer's Gift Shop in Honolulu.

1937 departure for Japan

Bombed Boat Arrives Here September 10

The Dollar liner President Hoover, raked by bombs dropped from Chinese planes yesterday while approaching Shanghai, will arrive in Honolulu September 10, a week from Friday, it was announced by Stanley Good, manager of the local office of the Dollar line.

The vessel, under orders of Admiral Harry E. Yarnell commanding the Asiatic fleet, did not go to Shanghai but proceeded directly to Japan instead, being able to proceed under her own power, although badly damaged, according to her skipper, Capt. George Yardley.

> "We are okay," was the welcome message Mrs. J. M. Dyer received from her husband, who with their daughter, Miss Betty Dyer, is aboard the President Hoover, bombed early yesterday by a Chinese war plane.

The liner has quite a few Honolulans aboard including a tour party under the leadership of Representative Yew Char.

In a wireless message yesterday from Char, shortly after the bombing, he reported that none in his party was injured.

Among those in the party are Mrs. John H. Wilson, wife of the postmaster here, and Mrs. Frank Locey, wife of the PWA administrator in Hawaii.

Char's party has had many exciting times while touring the Orient. They were in Peiping when martial law was declared in that city and escaped just before the Japanese invasion. They boarded the Hoover in Hongkong.

Newspaper account of the bombing of the President Hoover

JOSEPH B. POINDEXTER
GOVERNOR

TERRITORY OF HAWAII
EXECUTIVE CHAMBERS
HONOLULU

June 23
1939

TO WHOM IT MAY CONCERN:

          This will introduce MR. JOHN MICHAEL DYER, an American citizen who has resided in the Territory of Hawaii for many years.

          Accompanied by his daughter, Miss Laura E. Dyer, Mr. Dyer is making a trip around the world and any courtesies extended to them by officials of the countries through which they may travel will be appreciated.

signed
Governor of Hawaii

Governor Poindexter's letter of introduction

DIVINE WORSHIP
U.S.S. BOUNTIFUL
EASTER SUNDAY 1944
UPPER DECK, AMIDSHIP

0845 CHURCH CALL AND RAISING CHURCH PENNANT

0900 CATHOLIC MASS -- CHAPLAIN FITZGERALD

1000 PROTESTANT WORSHIP - CHAPLAIN SPARLING

CATHOLIC CONFESSIONS WILL BE HEARD SAT. APRIL 8, 1630 -- 1900 IN THE CHAPLAIN'S OFFICE, LOCATED ON THE PORT SIDE FORWARD ON THE MAIN DECK

All passengers and all ship personnel not on actual duty are urged to attend.

Service sheet on board ship in 1944

The fifth grade queen of the May and her court! I'm front row left. Babbie is in the square middle of the back row. Marcella is in the second row without a hat. Squease is

standing on the far right. Marney is the smiling one in the third row. Leslie is at left, all in black.

Bishop Hall, Punahou Elementary School

Royal palms at Punahou School

Graduation from Stanford, 1943. Nancy Darby on right

The house on Crozier Drive at Mokuleia

"From Here To Eternity" beach

King Kamehameha's statue in downtown Honolulu

Squease Weller on her convertible in my driveway

Eve Bruckner and the car I bought from Egghead for $35.00

CHAPTER 16

Around the World

*"One could barely see the eerie faces of men
on their way to war."*

Nineteen thirty-nine arrived, and it was time for graduation from Punahou. I designed my graduation dress and the same dressmaker made it for me. It was floor-length white sharkskin with slender straps and a little matching bolero jacket. Over the skirt I wore a white net overskirt. At one time I was the sweet girl graduate, and by discarding the net skirt and the jacket I became a tall dark siren, or so I hoped. My friends set me up with a date for the Senior Prom, and I had a reasonably good though unromantic time. After the ceremony our gang changed into our sailor *mokus* (long pants) and *palaka* shirts and set out to have real fun. We all drove to the beach and went swimming in our clothes and then we ended up going swimming in the fountain in the park across from the Honolulu Academy of Arts. That was to rinse off the salt water and sand. That was about as daring as one could get those days. We cavorted and laughed like crazy: no drugs and no sex as far as I was aware, and lots of carefree fun.

Only five of us from that Punahou class of 1939 of 119 graduates took the College Board exams. I had to be tutored in physics. I sweated out the College Boards, and then before finding out if I was accepted at one of my two choices for college, started out with my Dad for a pre-college trip around the world. Germany was a world threat, and rumors of impending war and of Jewish oppression persisted, but that didn't keep us home. Friends advised us not to go, but we were not dissuaded.

We sailed the end of June, 1939, on the Matson liner *Mariposa* for Australia via Samoa, Fiji, Pitcairn Island, and New Zealand. Daddy was a marvelous traveling companion. He wore his dinner jacket every night and waltzed me proudly around the ballroom.

After daylong stops in Auckland, Wellington, Melbourne, and Sydney, we left the *Mariposa* and sailed for Naples, Italy, aboard a P and O liner, the *Orontes*. She had British registry.

What a marvelously romantic ship! Only one hundred passengers, a small canvas-lined hold swimming pool, a full-sized tennis court, many deck quoit games and shuffle board areas, plus a very friendly bar where we played darts with the young officers every evening before dinner. I was the only young girl, and so I was the belle of the ship. Daddy and I were the only Americans on board.

England was two months away from the start of World War II. It was a heavenly hiatus for all of us. We dressed for dinner every night and we had dancing or movies. We sang "God Save the King" along with the rest of them. Under my breath I was thinking "My Country Tis of Thee." For movies we had *The Thief of Baghdad* with Sabu and *Algiers* with Hedy Lamar and Charles Boyer. Grand stuff. We saw each of these movies several times because we were

Around the World

on the *Orontes* for a whole month.

From Sydney we went around South Australia to Adelaide and on to Perth. We sailed the Indian Ocean to Ceylon (Sri Lanka). We anchored in the small harbor and were taken by launch to the dock.

I had seen beggars in China, but the streets of Ceylon in the poor districts were shockingly and unforgettably poor. When I hear of Mother Teresa taking care of the *poorest of the poor* I think of Ceylon.

People were lying sick in the streets and dying. There with no one to help them. I could look into huts where families lived and could smell the smell that only poverty emits: a combination of the smell of dead rats and human waste. The heat only added to the oppressive odors. The children were mostly unclothed. For a young relatively well-off American girl it was confusing to understand how I could be so well fed and clothed and these people could be so dismally poor.

I was learning about how some people are just born lucky or unlucky. It's the circumstances of birth. I'll never forget it, but unlike Mother Teresa I did not stay to help. We drove out into the countryside around Ceylon and I could see how beautiful it was. It reminded me of Hawaii with the green mountains and the palm trees and the blue ocean in the distance. I saw my first snake, as Hawaii does not have snakes. The snake charmer played his flute, and the cobra lifted its head and body out of the basket and weaved a little dance in time to the music.

We had taken on several passengers in Ceylon. They were English families who worked for the tea companies and were going home on leave. Actually, there were no older children, because they were all at school in England. Only the littlest ones were with us.

Daddy had made friends with a Yorkshireman, and every day they had several games of draughts (checkers) at a table set up on a lower deck next to the railing where they could play and also watch the ocean swishing by. After thirty days of this ideal existence Daddy one afternoon announced to me that he was going to his cabin to have a baath! My Yankee father had picked up an English accent.

Aden was amazing. Perched on the edge of the desert and at the entrance to the Red Sea, it was said to be the hottest place on earth. On the dock at Aden there must have been a hundred Ford touring car convertibles. Beside each one was a driver hoping to be hired. I couldn't believe my eyes. My absolutely all-time favorite car (remember Jimmy Castle's car?), and there were dozens of them lined up on the dock.

We hired one and took off on a tour of the desert. The Arab driver spoke some English, but there was really nothing to see except huge sand dunes and winding roads. He told us the joke about Cain being buried there because Aden was hotter than hell!

After Aden we sailed up the Red Sea. They filled the pool, and I swam in the sun without a *topi* (sun helmet), and my silver bracelet turned black from the salt in the water. That night I got very dizzy and nauseated and had chills and I was told by the doctor that I was suffering from sunstroke.

Also about this time I had another first experience. Two of the Aussies on board were single men, and I loved to play darts with them. One night they sneaked me a gimlet

Around the World

(gin and ice and lime juice) while my Dad was not looking, and I slurped it up and they handed me another. I slurped that up too, and pretty soon I began to feel very woozy and dizzy and soon I was telling Daddy that I didn't think I felt well enough for dinner. I don't think he suspected what was wrong. I fled to the safety of my cabin and stayed there the rest of the night feeling very foolish to have been such a dope.

When we docked at Port Said, we drove to Cairo and then out to The Shepards Hotel, where we had lunch and later a camel ride to the Pyramids. We had visited the Cairo mosque in the morning and had walked out onto the vast terrace where off in the distance one could see the Sphinx as well as the Pyramids. Daddy was offered dirty post cards. I remember the sleazy man who was peeking at them and leering at us.

We also walked through the Egyptian Museum and saw the mummies and the scarabs and the gold. It went on and on. And the bazaars! I bought some perfume from the perfume maker. He said the name of it was Virgin Mary's Hands. It was sickeningly sweet and I never ever wore it.

From Port Said we sailed into the gorgeously blue and cool Mediterranean. It was fantastic after the hot and extra-salty Red Sea. We swam again, and this time no sunstroke.

Our next and our last stop was Naples, and after a month on board we said goodbye to all the officers of the ship and to the sisters (nurses). They gave us a photograph of the ship's roster, and one of the sisters gave me a gift. It was a small wooden elephant with the upraised trunk, about five inches high. It was the end of July 1939. We didn't know that in September England would be at war and the *Orontes* would become a troop ship. An era was ending.

Once we got off the ship Dad went to the Wagon-Lits Office and booked our trip through Italy and then to Budapest, Vienna, Paris, and London. We had hoped to go to Berlin, but a war correspondent in Budapest warned us that Hitler's Germany was not a welcoming place for a young American girl wearing lipstick. Germany, he told us, was preparing for war and was on an austerity program. He didn't speak of the organized deportation and massacre of the Jewish citizens of Germany, at least not to me.

We had seen large uniformed groups on the various train stations while we were on our way from Italy to Hungary. Sometimes the train would just blow a shrill whistle and rush through the station without stopping. Looking out the windows we could see the soldiers lined up and waiting. The mood was solemn. War had not been declared, but they looked like they were ready to serve. We had not read an English-language newspaper for two weeks and were really out of touch with the negotiations going on between England and Germany. We were in our own tourist world.

Our hotel in Budapest was on the Buda side. It was near the bridge, and we could see Pest on the hill across the river. We had heard that Hungarian women were international beauties, and it seemed to be true; beautiful blonde women with great style and slim figures and charming voices. I was fascinated. I had never seen women who looked and sounded like that.

Around the World

On the way to Budapest we had gone to Vienna and had another enormous hotel room. We went to the opera and out to dinner in the park at a place called Kursalon. It was very memorable because the restaurant orchestra played Viennese waltzes and I floated up to heaven. It was like hearing "Aloha Oe" while looking at Waikiki Beach with Diamond Head in the background. Corny? You bet, and wonderful too!

By the time we took the Orient-Simplon express train to Paris from Italy, the number of soldiers had increased. At every stop along the way when we would lean out the window and buy coffee and rolls with butter and apricot jam, there would be hundreds of men in uniform.

We crossed the Alps in late August in a raging thunder and lightning storm. Every time the lightning lit up the sky, I could see the snow-capped mountains or the lakes. I couldn't sleep from thinking about the possibility that war was coming, and here we were a long way from Waikiki.

Dad had booked us into a hotel right around the corner from the American Express Office and the Paris Opera. He had canceled all the original hotels that he had booked in Naples because when we had arrived in Rome it turned out we were booked into a *pensione*, and my Dad definitely did not fancy staying in a boarding house. We had stayed one night and then moved into the Grand Hotel in Rome. I can only assume that he upgraded our hotels from Rome on because every room was palatial and seemed to be well located too. He was giving me, as he said, "*a trip you will never forget.*"

Many years later I realized that I had been spoiled, and it took me until my husband Jim and I went to Scandinavia in 1982 before I got over thinking I had to have an immense room with a huge bathroom.

I finally got unspoiled enough so that today I can happily book into a room without a bath so long as the location is near the harbor where we have a view. We have stayed in some memorable hotels where the bath was down the hall, but the ocean or the harbor was right outside the flung-open window.

So far I have never bumped into anyone on my nightly visits to the loo. I did have one funny experience though. In 1989 I stayed in a hotel in Florence where my bath was down the hall. During my bath I felt so euphoric that I burst into singing "O Mio Bambino" and almost immediately someone pounded on the wall to shut me up!

The two nights Dad and I spent in Paris on the last nights of August 1939, our sleep was disturbed by trucks rumbling past all night long. I couldn't sleep, and so I got up and looked out the window. The trucks were filled with men in uniform all standing up so that more soldiers could be packed in.

It was dark outside, but the trucks used blue headlights to light the way, and one could barely see the eerie faces of men on their way to war. No one was singing. It was deadly serious.

We left for London the following day. After having Dad as my roommate throughout Europe, it came as an ugly shock to find out that in England we could not legally room together, even though we were father and daughter. I was over the age limit of thirteen. No amount of foot-stamping did any good, and so we were given adjoining rooms on the same floor but without a connecting door. I

Around the World

was feeling very uneasy about being alone with the possibility of bombings during the night. I had experienced that already and knew how frightening it could be.

That day, August 31, 1939, the huge barrage balloons were being raised hundreds of feet in the air over Hyde Park and around the city. They hung over the city as a grim reminder that London was in grave danger of being attacked from the air. The headline in the *London Times* blared HITLER INVADES POLAND. It was just a matter of hours until World War II would start. The *Daily Telegraph* headlined BRITAIN'S LAST WARNING, but Adolph Hitler was a madman determined to carry out his plans for European domination despite Allied warnings to cease.

The fog was everywhere that night. You could hear the cars creeping by but you could not actually see them. You could stand on the curb and not see anything before or behind. We could barely see each other.

Friday morning, Dad made a quick decision to see if he could get us on the *Empress of Britain*, which was departing Southampton Saturday noon. We stood in a long line in the Canadian Pacific office, and when it was our turn we got the last cabin available for the next day's sailing.

With our tickets in hand we hailed a taxi and spent the rest of that Friday, September 1, 1939, having the cabby drive us to all the famous sites in London, Westminster Abbey, Buckingham Palace, The Tower of London, Parliament and Big Ben and Madame Toussaud.

We were staying at the Cumberland Hotel by Marble Arch. Pop loved to hear the soap box orators at Hyde Park corner.

The newspapers were filled with photos of the children

of London being evacuated and hanging out the windows of the train with their coats and little hats on and their lunches in their little bags and tears of despair at the suddenness of the change in their lives. Their mothers clung to their outstretched hands as long as possible.

The *Daily Telegraph*, September 2, 1939, reported that "a total of 300,000 children were transported yesterday from London to safe areas." Eventually 3,000,000 children would be sent to safe areas, some to America, to live while the war was raging.

We sailed at noon Saturday, September 2, 1939. We were going back to our own country and getting out of England on the last ship before the bombing began. At the very last minute, Pop had to buy some of his favorite English aftershave cologne. I thought for sure we would miss the boat!

Crossing the Atlantic, we had blackout covers on all the railings and the area above the railings, as well as all the windows and portholes. The ship steered a zig-zag course. Were we scared? Definitely. But we were young and there was plenty of light and dancing going on inside the ship.

There were rumored to be German subs about. Another ship, the *Athenia*, had left from Ireland the same time we left Southampton and had been sunk. We were given the news in the ship's paper. We felt an undercurrent of unease as we spent our days playing cards and our nights dancing.

My poor Mother back in Honolulu did not know we were on the *Empress of Britain*. For all she knew we might have been on the *Athenia*. We could not wire her until we docked at Quebec ten days later.

The English people with whom we shared a table were

Around the World

charming as usual, but they irritated us by maintaining the United States would be in it too before long. We stoutly denied that the war was our war. How little we knew.

One of the young men aboard was an unforgettable character. His name was Ludwig Von Hemfstangl. He was a son of Hitler's former foreign press chief. He and his father and his mother and the rest of the family had escaped from Germany to England in 1938. His father could read the handwriting on the wall, as the saying goes, and the family had agreed to leave by the only safe method. They walked out! They separated and each went his or her own way, and many months later they were reunited in London. Ludwig wore his souvenir of his days in Hitler's Youth Group. He wore a large brass belt buckle with a swastika on it. We corresponded for two years. He used to write to me from Harvard in code, and I would spend hours trying to break the code. He was too old for me though and I was not truly attracted to him except that he was so different.

We finally got to New York City the long way. The ship had gone down the St. Lawrence River to Quebec, and then we went by train to New York City. We stayed at the Taft Hotel and went to the World's Fair.

This time there was no flea circus and no Sally Rand, but there was something just as good: Eleanor Holmes and Billy Rose's Aquacade. It was a marvelous water ballet show, and we lined up with everyone to see it. I saw my first Broadway show and fell in love with New York City. The show was Ethel Merman in *Red Hot and Blue* and I also saw Gertrude Lawrence in a Noel Coward comedy, *Blithe Spirit*. I loved it all. We went to Dinty Moore at night for dinner, and I ate my first sidewalk hot dog, a Sabrette. Daddy was in heaven too because he is, was, and always would be a big-city guy. It was wonderful to feel safe again away from the war zone of Europe.

Five years later I would spend the morning in a sailboat off Waikiki with Gertrude Lawrence singing and laughing. Her nickname was *Gimo*, and she was a friend of Kevin Wallace of the San Francisco *Chronicle*. He was a friend of mine, and he called me one day and said if I'd bring down some eggs, I could have breakfast with Gertrude Lawrence. She was staying in the Wilders' house down by the Halekulani Hotel and was on her way to the South Pacific to entertain the troops.

During our breakfast she entertained us by relating the story of how she went to the beach at Normandy in a landing craft a few days after the invasion. She went to do a show and she said that as she was arriving on the beach in the landing craft, she was waving her black silk brassiere to the troops! There was thunderous applause from the beach. As I remember, Kevin cooked the eggs, while I tried not to embarrass myself by staring at this fabulous star of so many musicals. She had a marvelous sense of fun, the most sparkling eyes and widest smile and a wicked laugh. I was agog. I couldn't speak.

Later on, I bragged to my boyfriend from Boston that I had had breakfast with Gertrude Lawrence, and he replied, "Who's she?"

CHAPTER 17

On My Own At Last

"I may have been a blind date but I wasn't stupid!"

From New York City, Dad took me to South Hadley, Massachusetts, and enrolled me at Mount Holyoke College, definitely not a Catholic college. It was founded in 1837 by Mary Lyon as a Female Seminary. It would probably be considered nonsectarian. We had a large percentage of super smart Jewish girls from New York as well as super smart girls from all over. I think the college took me in because I was from Hawaii and they liked a geographical mix. My brains were not a factor.

I was almost free from parents and could hardly wait for my Dad to leave so I could buy my first pack of cigarettes. He saw me settled in my room and felt happy and proud that his little girl was enrolled in a fine Eastern College. His little girl was dying for a smoke, and so as soon as we had hugged good-bye, I hurried down to the store and bought my first pack of Chesterfields. During my high school days I had promised my Dad I wouldn't smoke again. In fact he offered me a thousand dollars if I would promise *NEVER* to smoke again. (I had been caught smoking by my mother's friend, Clara). I turned that down, but

I did promise I would not smoke again while I was in high school. As for college, there were no promises.

It was marvelous to be free at last of all parental supervision. Of course, there were rules to observe at Mount Holyoke, but rules were made to be broken. Right? *Right*!

There were rules about drinking and smoking and staying out too late at night. In order to overcome the rule on drinking, we would walk to the bar at the edge of town about two miles from the college, and then one of the older girls who had the most nerve would buy the beer, and I would spread my extra large and heavy fur coat on the snow, and we would sit on my coat and have a mini party feeling oh so wicked.

Each dorm had what was designated a smoking room. We were not allowed to smoke anywhere else in the dorm or on campus. It stunk to high heaven, and one needed a gas mask to go in it, but we thought smoking was cool and only the really *in* girls smoked. We played bridge, cut classes, listened to Frank Sinatra sing "Frenesi", and puffed away and played bridge. Once in a while we even studied.

We were supposed to be in the dorm by 11:00 P.M. on weekdays and midnight on weekends. This was not a bother to me because I wasn't dating anyway. Not that I didn't want to date. I just didn't know anybody and it was an all-girl school. Twice a semester one could have what was known as a two-thirty, which meant one could stay out until early morning.

Actually I had two dates that I can remember in the two years I went to college there. My first date was with a very handsome man from Amherst. He belonged to a fraternity and his last name was Ingram. His favorite song was "There'll Always Be an England" and he substituted Ingram for England. We went with a large group of his fraternity brothers and their dates from Smith and Mount Holyoke to a large playing field where we exerted ourselves playing baseball, drinking beer, and then back to the fraternity house where couples paired up and wandered off. I was his blind date. He took me up to his room and opportunity knocked again. He told me he had a condom, and I honestly didn't know what he meant and what it was, but I was beginning to be very wary. He told me I couldn't get pregnant. I may have been a *blind* date but I wasn't stupid!

My one other date was with a guy who must have been seven feet tall. He was very self-conscious about his height and that made me self-conscious about my height and neither of us was able to talk about it and laugh it off. I never saw him again either.

By the time June 1940 arrived, I had been to New York City several times and loved it. I rode the train and stayed on the college girls' floor at the Biltmore Hotel right near Grand Central Station. It was easy. You just walked up to the front desk and picked out the right color card for a college rate and registered. Each floor had a matron/watchdog, and no men were allowed on the floor.

I met Marcella Mahony from Punahou there one year and we both bought new bras at a fancy store on Fifth Avenue. I'll never forget how the saleslady had us lean over and adjust our bosoms into the cups of the bra, and then when we stood up we were amazed at how we stuck out and finally had a figure. We giggled and were delighted with our new profiles.

The war in Europe did not really affect us freshman girls. There was an uneasy feeling that the U.S. might get involved sooner or later and we discussed Lend Lease and read *The New York Times* and were horrified at the stories of Nazi atrocities. Some skeptics didn't believe the news articles and thought they were contrived to get us into the war. The girls who could knit kept busy making socks and mufflers, but the war was still *over there*.

When I arrived home in June, 1940, I had barely $15.00 in my pocket. When Aloha Tower, was finally in sight, I felt a thrill to be home again. It had been a year since Dad and I had left to go around the world. Honolulu looked as gorgeous as ever. The tug had come out to meet us at Diamond Head, friends had ridden the tug out and flung leis around our eager necks. The fragrance of the flowers, the sight of Aloha Tower, and the sound of the Royal Hawaiian band playing from the pier all told me I was HOME AT LAST! What a feeling!

Riding the tug out to meet the boat was possible back then. All you had to do was get down to the dock a couple of hours before the boat was due to arrive, pay the fare, which as I recall was $3.00, and hop on the tug. If we were meeting someone really special we'd buy a ginger lei for $1.00 and three strands of pikakes for $1.50. If we didn't know anyone coming in, we'd get three plumeria leis for fifty cents just in case we needed them. The tug delivered the pilot who would guide the boat into the harbor. When the tug got to the boat, which was waiting for us off Diamond Head, we would climb up a few rungs of the ladder and enter through the baggage entrance. We'd go to find

On My Own at Last

our friends and throw the leis around their necks and then enjoy the ride into Honolulu Harbor. It was gobs of fun to just pretend we were tourists arriving for a visit. We'd wave to our friends on the dock, and they'd play the game too and holler up, "Did you have a nice trip?"

I looked down at all the faces on the dock that June of 1940. Leslie Long was standing there waving and pointing to a tall handsome fellow standing next to her and then pointing up to me and then laughing. Leslie had been a good buddy of mine at Punahou. She was being a matchmaker, and the fellow bowled me over completely. He was Bill Brophy, and I was crazy about him from that moment on.

I had a very romantic summer, a summer just made for an eighteen-year-old girl. Bill was Catholic and wouldn't have dreamed of offering me the *opportunity only knocks once* line. He was brother to five fun-loving sisters, and my connection with his whole family from then on was very special. I learned to play their favorite game, cribbage, and I spent many happy Sunday suppers with them. So much more was happening at their house than at my house. My brother was in law school at Harvard. My folks might have missed me, but they were good sports and never complained. When I left to go back to college in September, Bill and I promised to write.

During my sophomore year at Holyoke I had made up my mind to transfer to Stanford University where there were men students. The only problem was my grades were terrible, mostly C's and D's. I had been having too good a time. Stanford would accept me for Summer Quarter 1941 if I could get my grades to a B average. That was going to take a lot of work, but I knew I could do it. Finally, I began to really study, and my folks were getting what they were paying for. It felt good to have a purpose. I was feeling good about myself and my ability to succeed. Bill had written a few times, and I was looking forward to seeing him.

I rode the train from Massachusetts to San Francisco and enrolled at Stanford in June, 1941. Instead of *The New York Times* I began a long affair with Herb Caen and the *San Francisco Chronicle*. We continued to read about the war and about the draft for the men (boys) and to speculate about whether our country would have to become a part of it.

I made reservations to sail home to Honolulu in September 1941 on the *Matsonia*. There was a slight feeling of uneasiness about crossing the ocean with a war going on in Europe, but we made an uneventful crossing. My vacation was about to begin at last.

Leslie Long (now Pietsch) met me on the dock again, but without my friend Bill. She warned me that I was in for some kind of disappointing surprise, and that I'd better be prepared. I wasn't sure what she meant, but I knew she wasn't being flippant. When an invitation came for a cocktail party, and when Bill didn't call me to ask me to be his date, I felt a warning signal. My cousin Mary's boyfriend, Ken, was undoubtedly the handsomest man in Honolulu. He was about 6'3" built like a surfer, lean and broad shouldered, hair bleached from the sun and a smile and a tan that topped off his extraordinary good looks. He was an older man, about thirty. Cuz said I could borrow him for the night. He was really a hunk, and he was my shield against what I knew in my bones was a major disappointment coming my way.

We made our entrance deliberately late. I had told Ken what I figured was going to happen and why I needed his support. He was enjoying playing the game with me. All eyes were on us as we entered the large foyer at the Weller house. I didn't exactly strut, but I was that close. Instinct told me why we were all gathered there, and instinct is always right. Squease Weller, a Punahou classmate, and my friend Bill announced their engagement! Leslie had warned me and I was almost prepared, but it still felt like a swift kick in the *opu* (stomach).

After the party, Ken and I parked up on Tantalus where we could see the city lights of Honolulu spread out below us. Opportunity knocked again. This time more urgently than ever, but once again I was able to lightheartedly suggest to Ken that he *look me up when I'm 30 and by then I'll be willing*. I had discovered my own line. My Mother had always told me that a girl's reputation was all she had, and once she lost it she couldn't get it back.

I spent a miserable fall of 1941 being heartbroken. This was my first experience with romantic rejection. I sat in the back yard and burned all of Bill's letters, and when the last page was still smoldering, I glanced down at the only word left and the word was *engagement*. I took that as a sign, and sure enough, a few months later, the engagement was called off.

That fall before the Pearl Harbor attack we were all dating young officers, and the sense that war was coming hung over us. Three weeks before December 7th, 1941, Barbara Brophy's fiance, Lt. Bill Kinney from Columbus,

Born and Raised in Waikiki

Ohio, was flying B-17's all around the perimeter of the Hawaiian Islands looking for the Japanese fleet. However, being in the Army Air Corps, he was not allowed to go more than 200 miles from the islands. Bill expressed his frustration at the inter-service rivalry that kept him from looking further out on his patrol missions. The Navy insisted on exclusive rights to patrol all of the ocean beyond 200 miles.

In mid-November, 1941 Bette Brophy's future husband, Herb Truslow, was called up by the Army to go on the alert. Herb and his troops camped out by Makapuu Lighthouse. They were out there to watch for the Japanese fleet and a possible invasion. This was a full three weeks before December 7th. There was no doubt in anyone's mind that the times were perilous and that war was imminent. The Japanese Foreign Minister was in Washington, D.C., talking to our government, but we were all uneasy.

We played a lot of cribbage, but we never stopped thinking about what might lie ahead.

CHAPTER 18

December 7, 1941

"We'd hear a truck coming from far off and wonder if it was a Japanese plane."

The moment arrived that changed all our lives in so many ways. December 7, 1941, was a gorgeous day in Honolulu. I awoke with a feeling of intense satisfaction that in another half hour I would be on the tennis court with the same handsome Ken. As I was waking up I could hear muffled booms in the distance, muffled because they were from so far away. My first thought was that the Navy was at it again. They had been having practice firings for some weeks. When the phone rang just before 8:00 A.M. it was Barbara Brophy excitedly saying, *"The Japs are bombing Pearl Harbor. Bill Kinney just called me from Hickam. They are bombing Hickam Field too."*

Heavenly Father! What a shock! I told Mom and Dad, and we turned on the radio and heard Webley Edwards, Honolulu's renowned radio announcer, saying over and over, *"This is not a test, this is the real McCoy. The Japanese are bombing Pearl Harbor. The rising sun has been seen on the airplanes. Everyone stay in your homes. All military personnel return to your base. I repeat, this is not a test."*

Born and Raised in Waikiki

We looked at one another and wondered what to do, where to go next and how to defend ourselves. We didn't have the answer to any of those questions. Pop was true to form and suggested we have breakfast and then go to Mass. So we sat at the breakfast nook and started to spoon the grapefruit when we heard a very loud whistling like a bomb dropping and then the ghastly explosion from a short distance away. We looked at one another with fear in our eyes.

All thought of carrying on and going to church was out of the question from then on. Mom telephoned our friends who lived on Alewa Heights, and we were told to come up there, away from the more vulnerable place where we lived, right next to Fort De Russy. We rushed around the house frantically stuffing pajamas into a suitcase, and Pop backed the car out, and at the last minute Mom flew back into the house and grabbed up the roast beef she'd planned to cook for Sunday dinner. I was shaking uncontrollably! This couldn't really be happening!

From our driveway, we could see the traffic moving on Kalakaua Avenue. It was very dramatic. Cars filled with men in uniform were speeding as fast as possible and honking their horns for other cars to get out of the way. Other cars were filled with families out for a leisurely Sunday drive through Waikiki. Now and then there was a car driven by an elderly Oriental, and it just poked along at twenty-five miles an hour. Obviously some people still didn't know what had happened.

Finally we were on our way to Alewa Heights. Alewa is on the side of the mountain just back of Honolulu. It is a popular place to live because it is cool up there. Bombs had

December 7, 1941

fallen in the McCulley area near Waikiki, and so we were stopped by the Civil Defense and had to take a different route. We could hear sirens all over town. My dad was driving, and frankly I have forgotten how we finally managed to get to Alewa but we did, and we were grateful to be away from Waikiki.

Our friends had a large telescope pointed at Pearl Harbor twelve miles away, and with a huge lump in my throat, I peered through the scope and saw the black dots that were the Japanese planes. I could also see the huge black columns of smoke rising from the burning ships in Pearl Harbor. It was still only nine o'clock in the morning, and the second wave of Japanese bombers were attacking. The third wave was still to come.

Auntie Nell and Uncle George welcomed us with comforting hugs, and Mom and I were assigned the maid's room in the basement. They didn't have a maid, and the upper floor had only two bedrooms. Thank God Mom was willing to stay with me, or I would have died of fright later on that night. There was that feeling of utter disbelief and utter helplessness. None of us were in the military or in the Civilian Civil Defense. We passed the time staring out the large picture window and looking through Uncle George's telescope and silently wondering, What next? We listened to the radio and were warned not to turn on any lights that night. The Civil Defense patrols would be out and Japanese spies and traitors were suspected to be everywhere. The Japanese fleet was expected to launch an invasion at any time. We just looked at one another and gulped.

I think Mom cooked the roast, because I am sure we were hungry, even though we were scared. That night we were sitting in the dark, when suddenly one of the lamps came on all by itself. We all cried out in fear and yanked the cord out immediately. Before we could calm our pounding hearts, there was a loud rapid knocking on the back door. A young man with a large rifle stood there shaking in his boots all the time screaming at us that we were breaking the law. We shouted back that we hadn't meant to and that the light had come on because it had a short. Fortunately, he accepted the explanation and went away. I think he was as frightened as we were. We breathed a sigh of relief but still felt unnerved by the incident.

Daddy and I knew we had to do something to keep us from being so frightened, and so we decided to have a game of cribbage. We took turns holding the flashlight. The game dragged on, but it was something to do. The others got some diversion from watching us play. It was a memorable cribbage game for more than one reason. Nothing to do with war at all. My dad got a *28 hand*. Now, if you play cribbage, you know that the highest count you can get is 29. Most remarkable, and in all the games I've been in since that fateful night, I have never seen a *28 hand* again, much less a *29 hand*.

Since it was total blackout and we were emotionally drained, we all turned in early. Mom and I shared the single bed in the maid's room downstairs. Around midnight all hell broke loose again because a squadron of American B-17's had flown in from California and the defenders at Pearl Harbor and Hickam Air Base had thought they were *the Japs* coming back and had fired anti-aircraft at them. None were downed, fortunately, but all the island was awakened and scared *shitless* by the firing.

December 7, 1941

December 8, 1941, my Dad drove to the Honolulu Paper Company store and saw Stanley Taylor who owned it and bought a roll of blackout paper to use to black out one of the rooms at our house in Waikiki. Dad also bought tape to do the windows at the store on Fort Street. When we finally moved back to our home in Waikiki later in the week, we were witnesses to trucks filled with bodies being taken to the mortuary on King Street. Shanghai all over again.

We answered the call to give blood at Queen's Hospital. We had no official duties, and so all we could do was stay out of the way. At night, we sat in Mother's blacked-out bedroom. It was the only room in the house where we could have lights on. Also, it had an air conditioner. We set up a card table and carried water and sodas and ice and the cribbage board and cards and the books and whatever else we imagined we might need, and got ready for the nights ahead.

We got so we could walk through the house in the pitch darkness without bumping into any of the furniture. The street lights were all out, of course, and the only outside light came from the moon. We would put the toothpaste on our tongue and then water on the brush and then do the job. In the dark we couldn't see to put the paste on the brush.

We'd sit in Mom's room with the air conditioner on and one eye on the clock, one ear on the radio, and the other ear listening for unusual sounds in the night. We'd hear a truck coming from far off and wonder if it was a Japanese plane. Daylight was always a relief. We'd made it through the night. This fear of invasion lasted until after the Battle of Midway in May of 1942. But the blackout lasted for a long time, and so did curfew. In the early months of the war, curfew meant only authorized people on the street after dark. Later, curfew was extended until 10:00 P.M.

Immediately after the war was declared, Honolulu had a military government (Martial Law) with complete power to run the islands. Civilians were issued gas masks. All of the paper currency was stamped with *HAWAII* on the bills, in case our money got into enemy hands.

But life went on. The Friday after the Pearl Harbor attack, my friend Mary Castro was married to Ed Fitzsimmons at Sacred Heart Church. The wedding was at 2:00 P.M. and we all had to remember to get home by curfew. It was a beautiful formal wedding with satin and bridesmaids. It did not let us forget that we were still expecting to be invaded by the Japanese.

At one time during the war, there were over a million men in the Army and Marines camping on Oahu and Maui, training and waiting to be shipped down to the South Pacific. We were the staging area for Saipan, Tinian, Guam, Tarawa, Guadalcanal, and the other islands where battles would be fought. The Hawaiian islanders opened their homes and their hearts to as many as possible. Some of the servicemen thought of Oahu as just a rock; others fell in love with Hawaii and planned to bring their families and come back *someday.*

As the days dragged on, I began to make plans to return to college if possible. Winter quarter at Stanford would be starting in January, 1942. I was expected to be there to register right after the first of the year. So I went to Castle and Cooke shipping office on Merchant Street downtown. It was jammed with people hoping to get on a ship to return

December 7, 1941

to the mainland. The newspapers had said that only people with a priority would get a ticket. I didn't know if that meant me, but I sure was going to try to get one. The military were running the shipping office too.

I met my Punahou friend Babbie Henshaw and she scoffed that I didn't stand a chance of getting a priority. I stood in line anyway and when I got to the general's desk, I pleaded my case that I was enrolled at Stanford University and was expected back there in January to complete my education. He stamped my priority pass and I waved it in Babbie's face on the way out and hurried over to buy my boat ticket. We were told to report to the pier Christmas morning.

Mom and dad were real troupers about letting me go. Their faith combined with their natural optimism allowed them to kiss me good-bye without a lot of foolish tears. It was scary to think of crossing the ocean during wartime, but I was eager to get back to a world without blackout. It never occurred to me to offer to stay home and help out in case of need. I was a month away from my twentieth birthday.

When we got to the dock Christmas morning, it turned out that there were three large white Matson ships all leaving at the same time and traveling in a convoy. We were the first ships to leave after Pearl Harbor. One had December 7th wounded on it; another had military wives and children, and the third, my ship, had a conglomeration of leftovers. These included, beside me and four college friends, Pat Morgan Swensen from Punahou, a touring circus group, tourists going home after a visit to the islands, and last but not least a round-up of prostitutes. At least that is what we were told. Pretty dumb, since the *working girls* would all be back in full strength by the time I went home again in 1944.

I went to my cabin. The ship had already been converted into a troop ship with bunks for six in a room which originally had two single beds. I could smell cheroot cigarettes and perfume. After conferring with the other college-bound girls, we five decided to haul our thin mattresses and our pillows and blankets up onto one of the decks and to sleep all together on the deck.

We stuck together like five fingers. It was winter, and the ship rocked and rolled across the ocean, contrary to the usual smooth crossing. The ships were three abreast, the *Mariposa*, the *Monterey*, and the *Lurline*. We had the light cruiser *USS San Francisco* leading us, and two destroyers, one on either side of the three big white ships. We were a dramatic sight as we steamed away from the islands. Many cars drove to Diamond Head and honked their horns to bid us aloha. People flashed their mirrors at us. We on board did not know what lay ahead in the 2200 miles between Honolulu and San Francisco.

The crossing to San Francisco took one week instead of the normal five days. Our days were a mess. Bored children and frightened and weary parents were everywhere one looked in the lounge. All the chairs were claimed and held by whichever family member was free to stand guard. All games had been commandeered by different families. It was almost a free-for-all. People showed their true colors.

For five college girls it was just a case of putting in our time. We had no real chores and no responsibilities. Just

December 7, 1941

line up to eat, line up to use the bathrooms, and the rest of the time walk around the decks. Every light source was blacked out. The promenade deck was shrouded along the rails. We felt safe as long as we stuck together.

Twice a day, the cruiser would catapult a plane, and it circled our ships for several miles around looking for submarines or other enemy ships. I guess we were a trifle uneasy, but I don't recall anything specific. Not like three years later the next time I crossed the Pacific, again during wartime.

When we docked in San Francisco, we were met by the press, since we were the first survivors to reach the mainland. I refused to be photographed until I'd had my hair done, and so that was the end of that. I did have my name in the *Chronicle* saying something totally inane. I'm ashamed to admit it.

That night we stayed at the St. Francis Hotel and were invited to celebrate New Year's Eve with some of the ship's officers who had rented a suite in the hotel. After about an hour of the party I decided that I'd better split while I could. *Opportunity* was knocking again, and I definitely wasn't answering.

CHAPTER 19

Graduation And The War Effort

"I nearly peed in my pants when I heard him fiddle his bow against his bent saw."

Looking back, I realize that if I had joined one of the sororities, my life would have taken an entirely different turn. I would never have met Jim Sorensen, for one thing. I was much too innocent to handle the big-time sorority life. I needed to break in very gently at Stanford. So I continued to live in the small dorms and liked the friends I made there.

My roommate at Stanford had an 8 × 10 photograph of my future husband on her dresser. He was in his Navy whites, and I thought he was just marvelous-looking. The two years we roomed together at Stanford, Jim never once came to see her. Consequently, when I finally met Jim in Honolulu in 1945, I felt he must be available.

Her name was Nancy Darby. She had been at Smith College for her first two years and had transferred to Stanford for the same reason I had, namely to go to a co-ed school and meet eligible men. Nancy was a fabulous roommate. I just adored her spunk and her good nature. We dated several Army fliers and had a marvelous time with them. When the summer of 1942 arrived, Nancy's family invited

Graduation And The War Effort

me to visit them in Troy, New York. My parents were relieved to have me accept their kind invitation since it was not possible for me to go to Honolulu during the war. Nancy and I took the train to Seattle, and then we boarded the Canadian Pacific to cross the continent. We figured it would take five days.

Our first big stop was Banff. We got off and hired a car and driver and went to the enormous hotel and had a swim and lunch. We were the only guests there. It was about to be converted to a recuperation center for Canadian servicemen wounded in the war. We drove past two Mounted Police and swooned at their handsomeness. We saw moose and elk, but we much preferred the Mounties. That evening we got back on the next train going East, and from then on we just got off and took our pictures at every stop. The conductor advised us to read the timetable whenever he saw us, and we eventually discovered to our joyful relief that it would only take three days and not five days to cross the continent.

When September came, Nancy and I packed our things to go back for our senior year. I romantically and foolishly left the most beautiful dress I have ever owned. My father had bought it for me in 1937 in Shanghai. It was an evening gown from Paris: lavender silk georgette with a cross-over bodice, bare back, and yards and yards of skirt that swirled around and around when I danced. I wanted her brother, my summer romance, to see that dress and never forget me. For all I know it may still be in that attic in Troy, New York.

In the fall of 1942 I really began to study and to like my work. I was a Speech and Drama Major with an English

Literature Minor. It was a great combination for me. I worked hard on school drama productions and made costumes and studied music and at the same time took classes in Shakespeare and French literature.

One of my professors, Hoyt Hudson, was a visiting professor from Princeton University, and from him I discovered the joy of learning and research. One day he said something to us that I'll never forget: "Music is a pure form of desire."

I thought that was a wonderful description of how I sometimes felt.

I loved doing props for plays. I can recall one play about an English junk dealer. My job was to get the props assembled and ready to go on stage, and I recall scrubbing out a filthy toilet which was one of the props and saying out loud, "*MIGAWD*, my parents are paying all this money to send me to Stanford and I'm cleaning a toilet."

Graduation from Stanford, June 1943, came and I applied for and was accepted at the NBC summer radio school in San Francisco. Mom and Dad got a special priority to come over on the boat from Honolulu, and at last they got to see one of their kids graduate from college. Afterward, they went to Massachusetts to meet their first grandchild, and I stayed in California to prepare myself for a career in radio.

Eve, a friend from my dorm at Stanford, and I lived in a little house off-campus. We had a marvelous summer. We got butter and meat under the counter from the grocer in Mountain View. It was still wartime with coupon books for butter and meat and certain other items. We had a lot of spaghetti parties and drank a lot of beer and laughed a lot

Graduation And The War Effort

and it was all quite innocent. The landlord wanted to evict us at one point, but we talked him out of it.

I bought my first car. It was a Ford 1932 navy-blue convertible roadster with a rumble seat. I bought it from one of our summer playmates. "Egghead" was on his way to join the Navy, and he needed to sell his car. He offered it to me for $35.00.

At last, I had my own wheels. It felt just great. Because of the war, I could not get back to Honolulu. The radio school had been a flop, and so I had to figure out what to do next. Eve was planning to move in with her mother in Westwood Village in Los Angeles, and they invited me to come down south and live with them.

I decided that I was interested in real estate, remembering my Mother's wheeling and dealing back in Waikiki. I signed up at a real estate school, and about six weeks later I took the test and got my California Real Estate Salesman's license. Now what? I drove my little antique Ford convertible to Beverly Hills and got out and waltzed into the office of The Bel Air Real Estate Company. They looked me over and said I could hang my license with them. No salary of course, strictly commission, but I was made part of the staff.

My duties were to comb the *Los Angeles Times* and to go call on all the *For Sale By Owners*, known as *fizzbos* in the trade. The first one and the only one I called on was a large two-story white house in Beverly Hills on Roxbury Drive. The walkway leading up to the front door seemed a half a mile from the curb where I had parked my little car. Finally, the door opened, and a maid in uniform quietly informed me that no one was home. I fled to the safety of my car and wondered, What the hell do I do now? It never occurred to me to ask the maid when would they be home or to try to make an appointment. I had a lot to learn about listing and selling real estate.

I remember an ad in 1943 in the *Los Angeles Times* that read: "Two-story Mediterranean-style house, five bedrooms, three-car garage, tennis court, swimming pool, $25,000!" Twenty-five thousand!

Eve and I were inspired by the song "Rosie the Riveter", a song that urged everyone to take off their fur coats and to get to work for the war effort and to give their man a full dinner pail. We roamed the factories around Marina del Rey looking for work but were told that we didn't have any skills. We protested that we had graduated from Stanford but the man doing the hiring would say, "Yeah, but what can you DO? Can you type and take shorthand?"

We saw a woman sweeping up the factory yard, and we said, "We can do *that*!"

And the guy squinted at us. "Oh, no you can't. You graduated from *Stanford*!"

One day we saw a sign on Sepulveda Boulevard near Marina Del Rey, and it announced HIRING. We wheeled the little blue Ford up to the main office and were hired on the spot. I was put on a giant punch press and Eve on another equally intimidating machine. My machine punched little one-quarter-inch holes in the six sides of the ten-inch long incendiary bombs. The bombs were made in the Midwest somewhere and then shipped to Harvil for the finishing holes before they were loaded. It was grueling work. For the first time I was rubbing elbows and exchanging laughs with a different class of people, the union

Graduation And The War Effort

working class.

I think we were hired because when they asked during our interview if I could play the piano. I said yes. So the first thing I knew, I was tapped on the shoulder one afternoon and invited to practice with the Harvil Aircraft Die Casting Orchestra. I was thrilled to get away from the monster machine but a little uneasy about how I'd do as a piano player with an orchestra.

I needn't have worried. There were five of us in all, a guy playing a saxophone, another one on the drums, a third one on the guitar, and the fourth one alternating between playing his comb and playing a saw. I nearly peed in my pants when I heard him fiddle his bow against his bent saw.

We were a team, and the next thing I knew we were hired to play for the New Year's Eve ball at the Elks' Club in Inglewood. We even had a torch singer, which, of course, is the role I'd have opted for but I was stuck on the piano. It turned out no one else was very accomplished either, but the Elks *were having so much fun* they didn't notice that we played "In the Mood" over and over again. I could bang that out like a real pro.

My take-home pay for the night was $35.00. Then we went to an all-night joint after the ball was over and ate hamburgers with chilie and fries. I kept asking myself how a little girl from Waikiki ever got mixed up with this tribe of wild people. The jokes they told, the affairs they had, and the innuendoes of promising alliances were enough to send me running to Mother. Opportunity was knocking all over the place! I decided I was out of my element, and after about three weeks of this I quit. It had been an education such as I hadn't had at Stanford. I didn't feel better than they were. I just knew that I was different.

Mom and Dad, meanwhile, had come back from their East Coast trip. They invited me to come stay with them for the holidays in San Francisco, and I was happy to be in their loving care again. Right after Christmas, I got a telegram from Eve.

"Come at once. Stop. Interview with Metro Goldwyn Mayer. Love, Eve."

I hurried back to Westwood, and together we went to Metro Goldwyn Mayer for our interview. We were being hired as messenger girls to take the place of the young messenger boys who had gone to war. This was more like it. When my turn came to be interviewed I was ushered into a very large room with three couches and two enormous desks. I could barely see the man sitting at the desk. He was chewing on a large cigar.

"Miss Dyer, do you want to be in the movies?"

"No, sir."

"Can you live on $19.98 a week?"

"Yes sir," I lied, and we were hired. I was thrilled, and so was Eve. We were told not to wear sweaters to work.

We joined the other messenger girls in the little waiting room (which had one window and a door) by the main entrance to the MGM Studio lot. We hung out the window and the door just to see who came through the main gate and in what kind of car. The stars swept through the main gate in limos. We parked our little Ford outside the gate.

One of the girls had lied about not wanting to be in the movies, and every time the director who had discovered the singer Deanna Durbin came in sight, she would stick

Graduation And The War Effort

her neck out the window and burst into song. It was funny and pathetic.

Eve and I kept our cool, except, of course, when Clark Gable was getting his hair cut or having lunch in the commissary. Then we'd pretend we had a message to deliver, and we'd tear out of the messenger room and saunter slowly past the barbershop and take a quick peek at Mr. Gable, or go and sit at the counter in the commissary and pretend we weren't spying on him. He could always tell we were watching him, and one time he actually looked me right in the eye and winked at me.

We saw the MGM lion in person. We saw a beautiful young girl barely visible in the back seat of a limousine, Elizabeth Taylor arriving to go to work filming *National Velvet*. We sneaked onto the set of Katharine Hepburn's *Dragon Seed*, and in between times, we delivered messages to every department. My least-favorite department was editing. The man's name was Weiner and he was a creep. I was supposed to pronounce his name as if it were spelled Wyner.

"Message for you Mr. *Weener!*"

He would roar at me. "*Wyner!* WYNER!"

Eve, on the other hand, was getting fanny pats and pinches whenever she delivered a message to production. These were the big guys who made the decisions, and Eve was a very attractive blonde with lots of sex appeal. She could have made a career out of working at MGM. The idea was that we were supposed to find the department that interested us, and perhaps we'd be taken on and trained.

Born and Raised in Waikiki

Well, it was a fun and exciting job, and I could have stayed and used my training as a Speech and Drama Major, except for one thing. I was homesick for Waikiki. So in March I quit and went back to San Francisco. I drove my little faithful car up the coast highway, picking up servicemen along the way to help pass the time and to help with the ten-hour drive.

I immediately got a job with American Trust Bank. I was another messenger girl, another boring job. Meanwhile I applied for a job as censor of mail in Honolulu. It was my only hope of getting to go home during the war.

CHAPTER 20

Waikiki Wartime Dating

"Honolulu had someone for everyone. It was a heyday for the unwed."

Finally, one grateful morning around 9:30 A.M., I received a phone call at the bank asking me if I could be on the wharf by noon in order to sail to Honolulu immediately thereafter. Boy, could I! I lit out of there and took a cab to my apartment, drove the car to the service station, sold it to the attendant for $50.00, packed my things and got to the dock in time. I was on my way home to be a censor, where I was obliged to work for at least one year.

We sailed on a hospital ship, the *USS Bountiful*. Once again we were on a run to Hawaii, only this time there were no Navy ships to protect us. We were all alone on a zig-zag course across the Pacific. It was going to take us at least ten days to make a crossing that normally takes five days, and always with the thought of Japanese torpedoes sinking us all.

We were a motley crowd of about 300. Six of us were single young women, and the rest were mothers with their children and their measles! This time I was assigned a bunk in a tier of three bunks in a very large ward room. This, after all, was a ship fitted out to carry patients, and so only a few had a regular bed. There were two enormous ward rooms with bunks for at least 150 people in each. The *head* consisted of ten toilets and three showers. Conditions were very crowded, to say the least.

The accommodations were below the water line, and with any imagination, one could feel a torpedo coming through the bulkhead and blowing us all up. For food we lined up like Navy hands and took a slotted tray off a large pile of still-wet trays. The steam pipes were overhead and the serving counter was small, and so we got out of there as soon as possible. The food was strictly Navy chow: lots of mashed potatoes, pork chops, gravy, canned beans, and coffee that could walk by itself. The amount of leftovers that were dumped over the side each evening was enough to feed several families.

There was a character on board whom I have never forgotten. She picked up sailors right and left, and when she showered, she left the curtain open and exhibited her body to anyone who wanted to look. She gave us lots to talk about, and the sailors walked through our ward often.

I, on the other hand, played a lot of bridge with three women I already knew from Honolulu. One had one of the private cabins all to herself. I was very envious, but able to overcome it because she didn't rub it in. Anyway, we set up a card table out on the promenade deck, and we whiled away the hours looking at our cards and then out to the deep-blue ocean looking at the flying fish. As the ship approached the islands, the ocean began to look like our beautiful Hawaiian waters, and we all exulted in our being able to go home.

Easter Sunday morning of 1944, I had the unique privilege of wheezing out organ music for the Catholic Mass and then playing hymns for the Protestant service. Being ecumenical long before it was popular, I got a lot of satisfaction from performing these small duties, though it was hardly a duty, more like an honor. Both church services were held out on deck with the blue Pacific swishing by. This time I made darn sure of how many flats or sharps there were in each hymn.

Finally the day came when we rounded Diamond Head and turned into Honolulu Harbor, and there was Aloha Tower! Since it was wartime I hadn't been able to tell my parents I was on the way home, and so for the first and only time, I got home without having anyone fling a lei around my neck.

I hired a taxicab and was driven to our house on Beach Walk. I'll never forget my mother's squeal of delight when she exclaimed *"Betty's home!"*

The next day I went to the post office building in downtown Honolulu and was interviewed, and received the censorship training from Mrs. Paty, Bill Paty's mother. She impressed on me that NEVER was I to reveal the secrets of the Censorship Office. It was wartime regulations. Bill had been a friend at Punahou.

After a couple of days of this indoctrination, I was ushered into a huge second storey room at the main post office and found myself working with about a hundred Honolulu women and older men. Most of the women were old enough to be my mother. They were great fun, and I enjoyed my year with them. They liked me too. I was so happy to be back home and to be employed at something I found interesting. I earned about $200 a month. My dad made me put it into savings bonds, and after my husband and I were married it came in handy when we built our first house.

We censors weren't allowed to compare letters, but once in a while we just couldn't help it. Most of the mail was very boring, but occasionally there would be a letter from a University of Hawaii professor or from a two-timing sailor. The professor wrote with great wit and style, and the sailor would write the same love letter to several women with only the girl's name different in each letter. It was very tempting to switch envelopes and double-cross the double-crosser. Once in a great while the letter would be so pornographic that we would suspect it was a code. Sometimes the lady who read it would have to go lie down for a while. We would giggle and poke each other in the ribs.

"Elaine must have gotten a hot one."

Mostly we read Merchant Marine mail, and most of the time we were excising places the ship was going to and the other information the writer was attempting to pass. We used our razors with caution, but with firmness too. No information on ship movements got by us.

Honolulu had someone for everyone. It was a heyday for the unwed. Women who had given up ever meeting someone in the remote Hawaiian Islands suddenly found themselves dating eligible men, and so the marriage license bureaus did a brisk business.

I had a marvelous year dating majors who were clerks in their civilian life and G.I.'s whom I'd known at Stanford. It was a crazy, wacky world. I learned to defend myself from the truly aggressive and to look out for myself in ways I'd

Waikiki Wartime Dating

have never imagined.

Julia Brown, a Honolulu society matron, acted as hostess for the younger groups of servicemen. Mrs. Brown had a list of eligible young women, and she would call and invite us to wherever the party was going to be. Most times it was fun, but one time it was a near disaster.

That night my friend Sue and I had agreed to go to a party for Marine fliers. The party was out at Malaekehana, way up at the north end of Oahu. We were told to meet the transportation at a designated spot on River Street. River Street! That was where all the thousands of servicemen lined up to visit the *working girls* and pay $3.00 for 3 minutes.

At five o'clock we met on River Street and laughed about what kind of a party this was going to be. We were willing to risk anything for a good time. I didn't know about Sue, but I was sure that I could handle any situation where "opportunity knocked." After all, I had so far!

We rode out to the country house where the fliers were, and when we got there we didn't like what we saw. Too much pairing off, and for sure, too many of the men were already quite intoxicated. I murmured to Sue that I was going to hitch a ride back to town with a jeep that was leaving immediately. She allowed as how she was coming too, and so we jumped in. There were two men in the front and three of us in the back. Another girl, also named Sue, wanted to go home too, and so she joined us in the back seat.

It was going to be a very long drive back to Waikiki where we three lived. When we got to the top of the hill by Hanauma Bay, we had driven all around the island from

Born and Raised in Waikiki

Malaekehana to Makapuu and Coco Head. The driver stopped, and I saw one of the men jump out. He apparently wanted to relieve himself. Meanwhile the driver seemed to be very busy with the lap of his pants, and I glanced over the front seat and to my horror I could see he was working his private part. I almost died of shock.

I managed to whisper to Sue what was going on and we made our plans. We were three against two so far, but when he let the first Sue out at her house it was going to be two against two, and after we let the second Sue out at her house, it was going to be two against one, me!

We were still about ten miles from town, and when we finally pulled up in front of the first Sue's house on the slopes of Diamond Head, we had made our plans. We threw our towels at their faces and leaped out and ran into the yard of a strange house. It was pitch dark. We huddled close to the sleeping house. After a few curses of rage, the men got back in the jeep and drove off. We were still shivering from fright, but we woke up the household, and the owner, who turned out to be a friend of my father's, called my dad and he came and picked us up.

Nothing was ever reported as far as I know. My mother gave me another stern lecture about my reputation. I didn't need any further warnings.

Sometimes Julia Brown would invite us to the beautiful old mansion in the coconut grove near Kapiolani Park. It was known as the home of Chris Holmes. It was at least two stories high and had an elevator. During World War II President Roosevelt came to Hawaii to meet with the war commanders and stayed at Chris Holmes' place. It was easily guarded, being next to the ocean and not having any

Waikiki Wartime Dating

other houses around it.

It was also used as a rest and recuperation place for Navy and Marine pilots. There would be about two dozen handsome young men doing their best to prove they could drink more scotch and gin and bourbon than the previous group had drunk. We would play pool, drink, have dinner, drink, sit through a movie, drink, and by nine o'clock I, along with the other girls, would be driven home. It was still curfew. I never had a serious romance with any of them. They were all very homesick and sadly in love with their girlfriends back home.

By the time a year had passed and I had had a marvelous time, as well as some scary times, I was more than ready to meet someone as honorable and as intelligent, not to mention attractive, as Jim Sorensen.

When the fateful day arrived, I was in the tub getting ready to go to a wedding when the phone rang. I dripped out to answer.

"This is Jim Sorensen."

I had been waiting for this. My friend from Stanford, Madge Weber, had written that she was giving my telephone number to Jim Sorensen. We agreed to meet the next afternoon at King Kamehameha's statue after I got off work.

I waited expectantly at the bus stop by King Kamehameha. Off across the vast parking lot by the post office, I could see a very tall, lanky Naval officer approaching. He was wearing a khaki uniform with a cap to match. He was smiling at me, and my heart went *ke-bump, ke-bump*. After we exchanged smiles we boarded the bus to Waikiki and got off at my house and walked in the front door and I introduced him to my Mother. We put on our bathing suits and walked to the beach, but not before Jim went to the Frigidaire and helped himself to a glass of milk. It was all so very comfortable.

We walked to the beach by what is now the Outrigger Reef Hotel. We got into the cool water and swam a little. I was intrigued, and I could tell he was too. We had a conversation about artificial insemination, and I suppose Freud would say that was very Freudian and it probably was. Still I was impressed that we were having a real conversation and I was learning something. Later on I introduced him to my father, and still later on, Daddy said to me these memorable words: "Now, *there's* a boy I could like!"

Jim was an engineering officer on the battleship *Mississippi*. She was having more guns installed on her decks in order to withstand a kamikaze attack. The Japanese were getting desperate and were sending pilots willing to die for Japan out to dive-bomb the ships. They rode their planes all the way down and crashed on the deck with their bombs attached and exploding. They called themselves kamikazes. It was a dreadful time for the United States Navy. Thirty-four U. S. ships had been sunk and 288 damaged by kamikazes.

Jim and I began a three-month period of dating while the *Mississippi* was in Pearl Harbor getting fitted. We did not even have a kiss for the simple reason that Jim had what the Navy called the crud on his lip. We'd laugh about it, and we'd hug and hug, but there was no kissing. Of course, Jim probably would have died before he would have told me *opportunity was knocking*. And through the good works of my guardian angel, I was still a virgin, though just barely.

Once in a while, another Navy officer I was dating would show up when Jim was there, and then there would be sparks, and I'd be grateful to the other fellow for making me look so desirable.

Just before the *Mississippi* left Pearl Harbor to join the rest of the fleet in the South Pacific, Jim said something like, "Well, it's been fun."

"Maybe it's been just fun for you but I really like you and for me it's been more than just fun," I replied.

I felt terribly rejected, and when his first letter arrived I read it and did not answer. His second and his third letters came and still I didn't answer. Finally, a letter arrived marked *Please Forward* but I was still in Honolulu.

At last, I answered and said I was leaving for San Francisco as soon as the war ended, and that I truly cared for him and hoped I'd see him again.

CHAPTER 21

Waikiki Investors

"A year or so later there was a hotel where
our house had been."

During the war, people who could leave were moving out of Honolulu and going back to the mainland to live and by the time I got home in April of 1944 the land grab was in full swing. People sold to anyone who had the money to buy. Mom had no one to help her with the apartments on Kuhio and she couldn't resist making a huge profit, and so during the war, she sold the Kuhio property to a local Chinese investor.

The Orientals in Hawaii were poised and waiting for their chance to acquire property, and in the Forties, they succeeded in buying into places and neighborhoods where they could not have bought before. Many had been born and raised in Hawaii, and so why shouldn't they? They pooled their money into what the Hawaiians call a *hui* (group), and they began to buy up property all over. It was the same way in the old days when they bought an automobile. Five plantation men would pool their cash and together they would buy a car and then pile in and take turns driving the car around. You would see them on a Sunday drive—two men in the front and three in the back,

Waikiki Investors

and the driver creeping along at twenty m.p.h.

Soon after I returned in 1944, Mom had a Mrs. Lam who wanted to pay $90,000 cash for the Beach Walk house and land. The night Mrs. Lam came over with a deposit check of $1,000 I was in shock. Mother almost immediately realized she had made a mistake, and when she asked us what we thought, Dad and I told her we thought she was making a huge mistake or words to that effect. Mom called Mrs. Lam and was able to back out since no papers had been drawn up. Nothing had been signed.

The next day Mrs. Lam came back to our house. Mother thrust the uncashed check at her, and Mrs Lam took it and that ended the sale of Beach Walk. We were all, including Mother, enormously relieved. Then the Lord brought us Julie Hayes.

I say that the Lord brought her to us, and I believe that with all my heart. Julie was a woman of the world, Italian by birth. She partnered with a man named Frank Colombo. Her mother came over from Italy and lived with them. I never knew her last name.

Julie stood very solidly at about five foot six. Her hair was dark chestnut, and her skin was very full and white. She was not slender, more on the voluptuous side. Her eyes were sparkling and dark and she wore her hair in a loose bun. Her voice was her most distinctive feature; it was full-throated and she laughed readily with a warm, wonderful sound. She dressed in loose-fitting silk print dresses and always wore stockings and high heels. She looked and sounded like a fascinating European.

I never got close enough to her to glean any knowledge of her past other than that during the war she had a husband who was in the Navy, and they had owned a house in El Cerrito across the bay from San Francisco. She was divorcing him and getting the house in El Cerrito as her settlement.

She liked me and I liked her. I admired her for her zest and her gutsy thinking, and she admired me for my family. Our kids all met her and warmed up to her. Julie had spunk and ambition. She worked hard, and when Mom and Dad left Honolulu for a year in 1945, they leased her the house on Beach Walk. With their permission, Julie operated a very nice dress shop in what had been our home. It was a very successful shop. My friends used to tell me that they had bought a dress in my living room.

After Julie's shop was such a success, she and Colombo approached Mom and Dad with the idea of somehow working out a long term lease on the property.

Julie wanted to sell her house in El Cerrito just across the bay from San Francisco to take the cash out of it and use the cash as a down payment on buying our apartments on Saratoga Road. The Saratoga Road place adjoined the Beach Walk property. I was asked by my parents to go to El Cerrito and give them an opinion of value on the house. After all, I had a real estate license and supposedly knew something about appraisal.

In fact, I knew very little, but I went across the bay and found the house and wired my folks that I thought it was worth at least the $10,000 Julie said it was worth. So they struck a deal, and Julie bought the Saratoga Road place and was on her way to her first million.

Shortly thereafter, an agreement was made with Julie and Colombo to lease the Beach Walk property for fifty

Waikiki Investors

years. Julie wanted to have a hotel built on the site. Mother was fascinated with Julie's chutzpa. It was the kind of risking that she possessed but had never been fully able to use. My brother's Harvard Law degree plus his own abilities enabled him to draft the lease. So the papers were drawn up and a lease was signed, and Julie was on her way. It was 1953.

Julie had to get the financing and the design and the contractors, but a few years later she had her hotel, and she called it *The Polynesian*. It is still there on the corner of Kalakaua Avenue and Beach Walk, where my house used to be.

I recall sitting in our back yard while all the planning was going on and saying to Julie, "Golly, Julie, if you could get the Campbell place next door you could have an even bigger hotel." She liked my thinking, and the next thing we knew she had made a deal to lease it too.

As Mother was her original benefactor, Julie put the elevator and the pool on our property and the rest of the hotel rooms were on the old Campbell property, eventually part of the Weill, McNamara estate.

Mother and Dad were very tolerant of Julie and Colombo's paying problems. At first they had a hard time paying the monthly lease rent. At the time, I recall it was around $600 a month. But my folks did not really count on that for their living, and so they let her have the time she needed in order to get all her other bills paid. They knew that she was good for it sooner or later. And she was. A year or so later there was a hotel where our house had been. We could ride by and gaze at the palm trees Mom and Dad had planted and look at the five-story hotel and

Born and Raised in Waikiki

wonder at the miracle that had come our way.

Eventually Julie and Frank sold the Polynesian Hotel and retired to Italy. The last time I saw Julie was the day of my mother's burial in 1968. Julie and Frank were there to pay their respects.

The hotel has been sold and resold and refinanced, but we own the land and the lease and the income has steadily increased. The little 7055-square-foot lot fronting the main boulevard of Waikiki, Kalakaua Avenue, is the equivalent of a gold mine or an oil well.

I have always thanked the dear Lord and my parents for their good fortune to have bought a lot in Waikiki instead of a more fashionable neighborhood, and to have held on to it.

And I have always thanked Julie Hayes for her part.

CHAPTER 22

World War II Ends

*"No more curfew, no more rationing and
no more travel restrictions."*

By early 1945 the American high command began to realize that in order to defeat Japan they would have to invade the Japanese mainland. We had bombed Tokyo as well as secondary cities in Japan continually since mid 1944 but Japan did not appear to be ready to surrender. In fact, their suicide bombers were relentless.

It is important to remember that the first time American planes bombed Japan was April 18, 1942. The leader of the squadron of B-25's was then Lt. Colonel James H. Doolittle, later General Doolittle. It was a huge morale boost to the Americans fighting desperate battles on Wake and Midway and Guadalcanal Island. The battles for Tinian, Saipan, Tarawa, Tulagi, Guam, and Okinawa and the Phillipines would follow. The Pacific islands were a vast battleground for Allied troops fighting to liberate the islands taken over by the Japanese. Remember, Japan had started her aggression policy when she invaded China and Manchuria in 1937.

Both my husband and I met General Doolittle after the war, and I want to tell you when his blue eyes looked into my eyes and he shook my hand, I felt something in my gut. This was a man!

After the Allies had recovered some of the islands that Japan had captured, it was possible to establish air bases closer to the Japanese mainland and to resume bombing Japan. In November 1944, 111 bombers attacked Tokyo. In December, B-52's launched their 5th attack on Tokyo. In February 1945, 334 B-29's launched nightfire raids. The war seemed to go on and on.

President Franklin D. Roosevelt died in Warm Springs, Georgia, on April 12, 1945, and his vice-president Harry S. Truman took command. Roosevelt had been president since 1932, the first and only president to win four terms.

History will probably list Harry S. Truman as one of our greatest leaders, but when he was sworn into office, he was an unknown quantity. He had a wife named Bess and a daughter named Margaret, and they all lived in Independence, Missouri, and he had been a United States Senator. Oh yes, he could play the piano, and before he went to the Senate, he had been a haberdasher in Missouri.

The war in Europe had finally ended in May 1945, and it was time to end the war in the Pacific. It was end the war or else have to invade Japan. It was estimated that a million American servicemen would be needed for the invasion of Japan, and God alone knew how many would be killed.

President Truman had character and guts, two very important parts of the whole person. It fell to him as President of the United States to make the momentous decision to drop the atomic bomb in order to *end the war.*

August 6, 1945, the first bomb fell on Hiroshima.

World War II Ends

On August 9, 1945, the second atomic bomb was dropped on Nagasaki.

On August 9 and 10, British and American carrier-based planes attacked Japanese airfields.

On August 9, Russia declared war on Japan, and invaded Manchuria, which Japan had seized in 1937.

On August 10, 1945, Japan surrendered, but not unconditionally.

On August 13, 1945, 1600 American aircraft bombed Tokyo.

August 14, 1945, Japan agreed to surrender <u>unconditionally</u>.

August 15, 1945 was declared V-J Day—Victory over Japan.

The war that had begun September 2, 1939, was finally ended. The war that Hitler and Mussolini and Hirohito had perpetrated upon the world was over, and the Allies were the victors. Fifty-three million lives were lost. Three million people were missing.

World War II was finally over.

On August 27, 1945, the US Navy steamed into Tokyo's Sugami Bay. It was the greatest naval display in the history of the world. There were twenty-three aircraft carriers, twelve battleships, twenty-six cruisers, one hundred and sixteen destroyers, twelve submarines, and one hundred and eighty-five other smaller ships. Admiral William (Bull) Halsey was the commander.

On that momentous day, engineering officer James Francis Sorensen had the smoke watch duty on the battleship *Mississippi*, which meant that he hung out at the top of the ship's mast. It was a fortuitous duty call, and with his binoculars he watched the historical parade of ships into Sugami Wan. From his perch at the top of the mast he described the scene to his shipmates down in the engine room. Communication was through a speaker tube that fed sound into the engine room way down below.

On September 2, 1945, the formal instrument of surrender was signed on the deck of the battleship *USS Missouri*. General Douglas Mc Arthur signed on behalf of the Allies. (United States, United Kingdom, Soviet Union, Australia, Canada, France, Netherlands, New Zealand). Foreign Minister Shigematsu signed for Japan. Admiral Nimitz signed for the United States.

There were hundreds of thousands of servicemen training for the invasion of Japan, and they and their families breathed a sigh of relief. The men who had fought in Europe also breathed a sigh of relief now that they knew they would not have to be shipped over to the Pacific.

We listened to the radio, constantly monitoring the progress of the surrender and wondering how soon it would be before our friends in the service could come home. I went around singing "Kiss Me Once, Then Kiss Me Twice." Another favorite song was "When The Lights Go On Again All Over The World."

When the surrender was finally a sure thing, Waikiki went wild with joy and relief! We ran around hugging everyone we met, friends or strangers, and playing music as loud as we could and singing and staying up all night celebrating. No more curfew, soon no more rationing and no more travel restrictions. The sense of relief was enormous. The dread of war no longer hung over us.

Everyone discussed what number their military friends

World War II Ends

and relatives had for getting sent home. All the servicemen had a number that indicated where they were in the rotation for getting shipped back to the States and released.

THE WAR WAS OVER! The men were coming home!

Mom and Dad and I began to make plans to go to the mainland, and since we were civilians we could make plans right away. I wanted to go to San Francisco and wait to see if I ever saw Jim Sorensen again.

Meanwhile, Lieutenant James F. Sorensen, USNR, was steaming through the Panama Canal on his way to the decommissioning of the *USS Mississippi*. The plan was for this to take place in the city of New Orleans. With all hands on deck and all pennants flying, she tied up at the dock in New Orleans, and the invitations to balls and tea dances poured in. It was heady time because not only was the war over, the men were returning heroes.

I was sure I'd never see Jim again, that some simpering southern Suzy-belle would sweep him off his feet.

Lt. James Francis Sorensen, USNR

Jim Sorensen when we first met in 1944

THE UNITED STATES OF AMERICA

IN RECOGNITION OF AN OUTSTANDING CONTRIBUTION
TO THE NATION'S WAR EFFORT

Certificate of Merit

HAS BEEN AWARDED TO

LAURA E. DYER

BY THE OFFICE OF CENSORSHIP

Director.

Certificate of Merit from the Office of Censorship

*Betty Dyer weds Jim Sorensen, September 28, 1946.
San Francisco, California*

*Jim Sorensen with our two dalmatians
in front of the house we built in Fresno, California*

Jim's parents Victoria and Bert Sorensen and Jim's sister Shirley and her husband Chuck Mansperger. The baby is Mary and it is Christmas, 1948

*Mary Rogers, our babysitter and friend,
holding Frances, 1951*

Duck hunter Jim, with Mary and Fran and three nice ones

Leaving Honolulu airport in 1953. My dad on the left and my brother Jack holding our current baby, Stephanie. Mary, Fran and Katy Dyer are standing in front of Jim and me

Drew, our fourth child and first boy

*Jim and the four children we had born to us in Orange Cove.
Drew, Mary, Stephanie, and Fran*

Our family is complete.
Baby Sally joins the rest of the gang in 1958

Mary, Drew, Stephanie, Sally and Fran, 1971

*601 North Encina Street, Visalia.
Our home from 1958 until 1976*

The Waialua Show
Words and Music by:
Laura E. D. Sorensen

Down in Waialua town is a place of great renoun,

people come from miles around to the Waialua show.

Different picture ev'ry night Philipino movies that's right!

Philipino Japanese and Chinese and Haolekine show at the

Waialua show, at the

Waialua show. You only gotta bring

your mosquito bomb plenty of popcorn and good ole Mom to the

Waialua show, to the Waialua show.

Phi-li-pi-no Ja-pan-ese and Chi-nese and Hao-le-kine show.
Way down Ha-le-i-wa wa-y dif-frent pic-ture ev-ry day
Phi-li-pi-no Ja-pan-ese and Chi-nese and Hao-le-kine show.
Dif-ferent pic-ture ev-ry ni-ght Phi-li-pi-no mov-ies
out-a-sight! Phi-li-pi-no Ja-pan-ese and
Chi-nese and Hoa-le-kine show at the
Wai-a-lu-a sh-ow, at the
Wai-a-lu-a sh-ow. You on-ly got-ta bring
your mo-squi-to junk, plen-ty of pop-corn and lots of punk to the
Wai-a-lu-a show. Oh to the Wai-a-lu-a sh-ow.

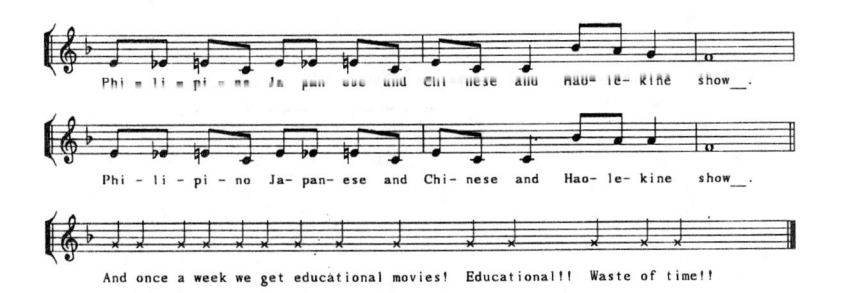

Phi-li-pi-no Ja-pan-ese and Chi-nese and Hao-le-kine show.

Phi-li-pi-no Ja-pan-ese and Chi-nese and Hao-le-kine show.

And once a week we get educational movies! Educational!! Waste of time!!

© Copyright 1972 Laura E. D. Sorenson

© 1993 Laura E. Sorensen

"The Waialua Show Song"

Honolulu Harbor, Aloha Tower, and the tug

The whole family at Wilsonia, September, 1994

CHAPTER 23

I'm Not Going to Be an Old Maid after All

"This husband had a lot to learn about female independence."

> *Last night we dined in Heaven,*
> *We feasted on the stars,*
> *We drank a cup of the Milky Way*
> *In all the Heavenly bars.*
>
> bds

Then followed a period of about eight months when Mom and Dad and I moved to San Francisco and later on to Los Angeles. The war was over, and we needed a taste of bright lights and no rationing.

In early 1946, Dad bought a two-story, four-apartment building at 817 South Normandy, about two blocks from the Ambassador Hotel in Los Angeles. Each apartment was identical—three bedrooms, two bathrooms, hardwood floors, and a little balcony. And the price for the entire building was $35,000. Dad paid cash, of course. I don't think he ever bought anything on time or with a charge card, except their first mortgage on Beach Walk.

Being in Los Angeles, Jim was able to come down and visit, and I was invited to Fresno to meet his family. I recall one weekend at their ranch on First Street. In the morning

I'm Not Going to Be an Old Maid after All

I was awakened by the crowing of a rooster—a lovely sound that reminded me of visiting Aunt Daisy on Maui. The next morning I missed the rooster's crowing and asked why I hadn't heard it, and found out we had eaten the bird the night before.

Jim's family accepted me and my different religion. His mother, Mary Victoria Cutten, was very faithful to her Presbyterian church, but Jim's father only went to church on Easter. I had long passed the point of no return on that matter. It was accept me as I am or don't accept me at all.

When I got married and lived in Fresno, I went to church regularly. It never occurred to me not to go, nor did it occur to me to require that Jim go with me. It seemed to run in Jim's family that the mother did the church stint and the father read the Sunday papers, and everyone was content with this arrangement.

And so after about a four-month courtship, Jim and I became engaged in May of 1946. He had been invited to visit us for the weekend. He came down to Los Angeles on the bus from Fresno, where he was working as a beginning civil engineer at the Fresno Irrigation District and living at home. We had tickets to go to an all-Gershwin concert at Hollywood Bowl. My mother cooked her great roast beef dinner, and then she and Dad discreetly left, and I made out as if I had cooked it all myself. Naturally, it was delicious since my Mom had been the cook. Anyway, after a mildly romantic dinner we drove to the Bowl with our blankets and sat under the stars, holding hands and listening to the wonderful music.

My thoughts were racing wildly. Is he going to give me my ring now? What is taking him so long! Did he forget to bring it? On and on. Later, after the concert, we sat in the moonlight on the apartment's little balcony, and again I was silently wondering. Is this the Moment? Still nothing. I was beginning to get frantic, and I had the feeling he was toying with me.

Jim had asked me to marry him on a trip to Pacific Grove earlier, and now I was about to get my engagement ring, but when? For God's sake, when? Finally, it was about one in the morning and the bus back to Fresno was leaving from the Greyhound Depot in downtown Los Angeles. We drove down to the depot and walked into the crowded station. I was feeling very disappointed. Suddenly, Jim put his hand into his pocket and pulled out a ring box. He was smiling all over with pride, but I was a bit chagrined that he'd waited through several romantic ring opportunities and I was finally receiving my engagement ring in the Greyhound Bus Depot! But it was kind of funny too, and we both laughed! I was now officially engaged.

Mom and Dad were very happy about everything. Jim was their favorite. His sense of humor matched theirs, and Jim showed my father the respect my dad deserved by formally asking for my hand in marriage. After Daddy consented, Jim jokingly and typically asked my dad to be sure my teeth were taken care of before we were married. In case I needed a filling.

We set a date for Saturday, September 28, 1946. The site would be Old St. Mary's Church in Chinatown in San Francisco. There was some goodnatured grumbling about having to miss the Berkeley football game, but we were wed, and friends came from Fresno, and from Los Angeles, and I had several friends living in San Francisco from

I'm Not Going to Be an Old Maid after All

Honolulu and Stanford, Lorraine O'Brien, Doris Wilsey and Madge Weber. We had our reception at the Fairmont Hotel, and Mother arranged for the small Hawaiian band from the Tonga Room to furnish the music. I even think I might have danced the hula. I know it was expected of me. I wore my hair up with a crown of white carnations. Jim wore a tuxedo. His sister Shirley was my one attendant, and a friend of Jim's whom we have not seen since the wedding day was his best man.

The moment before my Dad walked me down the aisle was a very precious time for me. I looked at my beaming father and felt so proud to be next to him and to have him take me down the long aisle to meet my future husband. I was not the least worried about anything. This moment was the one I had saved myself for.

We left for our honeymoon in a car borrowed from Jim's father, a 1938 green Ford coupe. I had my fur coat over my arm, my navy-blue wool suit from Magnin's, and a marvelous off-white felt hat with a huge red velvet bow. Jim wore his tweed jacket. For years afterward I wore that same hat to the Cal-Stanford game, and whenever Stanford scored, Jim's college friend Cliff Hull would bash my hat down over my eyes. All in good fun. As for Jim's jacket, he still has it and wears it.

We hadn't gone four blocks from the Fairmont Hotel when a crazy driver cut in on us. I rolled down the window and screamed out at the top of my lungs, "*L. A. driver!*" Jim looked at me in shocked bewilderment. He was seeing a side of his new wife that he hadn't seen before.

We had been advised by a wise friend to take champagne and sandwiches with us in the car as we drove off from the Fairmont Hotel down California Street. *"You'll be hungry in the middle of the night!"*

Opportunity was really knocking now, and since we didn't want to muff it due to the fact that we were grossly inexperienced, we took along a guidance book. We dubbed it the Blue Book.

After we had settled into our room at Brookdale Lodge near Santa Cruz and had carefully fixed the skimpy curtains so that they covered the windows, just barely, we took the book out of the suitcase.

I was wearing a beautiful satin night gown saved for the occasion and a white silk robe edged with lace. Jim dressed carefully in p. j.'s and a dressing gown. We were nervous but determined to do it right.

We sat on the edge of the double bed and opened the book to page one. We studied the book together for a few seconds. Then we looked up and looked each other in the eyes and found what we wanted to see, and we tossed the book away and followed our instincts.

The next morning after a well-deserved sleep, some champagne and sandwiches and some more practice, we discovered another important detail. We both liked to read the paper with breakfast. Whew! That was a relief, and probably one of the more important discoveries we made on the entire honeymoon.

We spent the third night of our wedding trip with Jim's grandfather Sorensen. Grandpa had a wonderful big house in Pacific Grove on Granite Street just about three blocks up from Lighthouse Avenue. The house had a special meaning for us, for it was in one of the bedrooms upstairs that we had gotten engaged.

I'm Not Going to Be an Old Maid after All

At the time it was all very innocent, of course. We were with a chaperone couple who were married, and while they were napping, we also napped, only we didn't actually go to sleep. This was about six months before we were married. Anyway, during our time in the bedroom Jim said to me, "Well?" and I archly replied, "Well, what?" and then Jim said, "Will you marry me?"

I accepted him of course and then I told him another of my mother's one-liners.

"I fell out of bed when he proposed!"

That afternoon we walked to the Pacific Grove beach and found a secluded place along the water, and I told Jim that I didn't care if we had a servant or not but I definitely wanted to have six children. He nearly choked. "SERVANT!! SIX CHILDREN!" he exclaimed but he didn't actually object, and so we were engaged.

That's partly why we chose to visit his Grandfather on our honeymoon. Grandpa Sorensen was a crusty Dane of about seventy-six years at that time so it didn't surprise me too much when the first morning we were there sitting around the kitchen table he declared, "Catholics worship idols."

Good Lord, I thought, this is terrible. I can't let this go unchallenged. I swallowed my food which had stuck in my throat and said as carefully as I knew how, "Catholics do not worship idols. The statues in the church are the same as the photographs in your house. They are merely reminders of the important people in our lives. The statues are reminders of Our Lord, of the Virgin Mary and of St. Joseph, etc."

End of discussion. It was never mentioned again. We piously told Grandpa that we were planning to save a lot of money. He humphed and said, " It's not what you save; it's what you DON'T spend!"

Grandpa was something of a tyrant, being of the old school, but he was very smart and had made excellent real estate investments and was very generous. One year he presented all his heirs with checks for one thousand dollars. I was included. At one time he had owned the corner of Shaw Avenue and First Street in Fresno where Macy's is today. He gave it to his son Leland and when the Depression came, it got sold. If he had held on to it and leased it, we would all be very rich and probably not nearly as happy as we are.

In his later years Grandpa Sorensen traveled to Mexico to go shell collecting, and his collection included shells from all over the world. He was in fact, a world renowned collector, a conchologist. He collected shells with the living animal in them. Consequently, his house smelled *pilau* (stunk to high heaven), because there was always a box of sand in his basement with the dead shells and the animal inside being eaten out by the ants and the odor wafting up into the house.

At one time in his travels he discovered a unique abalone shell. It now bears his name and is known as *Haliotis Sorenseni*. We in the family of course refer to it as *Halitosis Sorenseni*. One time when Jim was in the Smithsonian Museum in Washington, D.C., he had the thrill of seeing Grandpa's shell in a special glass case all by itself with a large sign explaining that this was a recent discovery by Andrew Sorensen. Grandpa was a man's man and he lived to be ninety-nine.

I'm Not Going to Be an Old Maid after All

Andrew Severin Sorensen had been born in Aarhus, Denmark. He came to the United States to avoid being conscripted into the Danish army. There was not a war on, but he just didn't want to be in the army, and so he came over and never went back. He dropped his middle initial when he realized his initials spelled ASS.

When grandpa died, the paper in Pacific Grove quoted him as saying he was leaving his shell collection to the museum in San Francisco and then his children wouldn't fight over it. That was Grandpa!

On our honeymoon I discovered that I was getting bored being driven around and not getting my hands on the wheel. Finally, I asked if I could drive and got a look from Jim that seemed to say 'Forget it. This is my job, and besides I don't trust you with my father's car.'

Well, that didn't stop me from asking again and finally I was allowed to get behind the wheel, and since we didn't hit anyone or anything, I was allowed to drive occasionally. Boy, this husband had a lot to learn about female independence.

Jim's parents had generously deeded an acre of land to us on the outskirts of Fresno. It was on Shaw Avenue about a mile and a half from their house on First Street.

We hired a carpenter to build us a house. Jim had helped the concrete man lay the slab floor and then Mr. Thompson built our house. Most people thought we were' crazy not to wait until things get cheaper' but we ignored them all and went ahead.

And nothing has ever gotten cheaper.

We designed it ourselves in a style known as California Ranch. It had a living room, 18 by 24 feet, with beamed ceilings and large 4′ × 8′ mullioned windows along the front and the back. The material was knotty pine. At one end was the fireplace with a desk built in on one side, and bookshelves on the other side. The kitchen was a long narrow corridor kitchen, with windows facing Shaw Avenue. I could wave at my friends as they drove by. The bathroom was in between the kitchen and the one bedroom. It was all ours, and we were thrilled to have it. We were very happy as newlyweds, and we exchanged a lot of dinners with our friends the Hulls and the Petersons. It was so much fun to cuddle up and to feel close to my friend and husband. I loved being married.

Before Mary was born in 1948, we added a very large bedroom, so then we had a two-bedroom house. We also added a guest room and bath in the carport. All in all, we had spent around $8,000, and we owned it free and clear.

In addition to all this we had black widow spiders. I was unnerved and briefly considered going back to Honolulu. Anyway, I telephoned to the farm adviser and told him with a sob in my voice, "I have black widow spiders, what shall I do?

"*Lady, get a 2 by 4 and kill 'em!*"

My parents stayed with us now and then. Ethelwynne Lewis came to visit from Honolulu. Jim Lambert brought a series of girl-friends for our approval. One of them managed to always look picture perfect—navy-blue linen dress and pearls, while I was buried in diapers.

Her name was Lala, and I could tell she was smitten with my husband. We girls can recognize the signs. That's when I decided if any woman ever made a play for my husband I would stick my foot out and trip her after I had

I'm Not Going to Be an Old Maid after All

poured hot coffee on her!

Married life agreed with us. Jim was advancing at the Fresno Irrigation District, and the Millerton Dam was under construction and we'd drive up and look at it. The various irrigation districts along the Friant-Kern Canal were contracting to build their own systems to distribute the water that would eventually come from the dam and flow in the canal. Some of the districts were hiring their own engineers and building their own systems instead of having the government build them.

One fateful Sunday morning we had a phone call. It was from three members of the Orange Cove Irrigation District Board, and they wanted to have a meeting with Jim at our house. So Harvey Chase, Oscar Orlopp, and M.N. Jensen drove to Fresno. I opened the door for them and they walked in and the first words to Jim were, "We need you."

I picked up baby Mary and left the house and walked across Shaw Avenue to Brook and Georgie Gross's house and told them, "We're moving!"

And two months later, New Year's Day 1949, we packed up and moved to Orange Cove, a little town forty miles east of Fresno and eighteen miles north of Visalia.

The ironic thing about moving there was that we had gassed up in Orange Cove while we were still on our honeymoon, and I had looked around the town and remarked to Jim something like, "Boy, I hope I never have to live in a place like this!"

I had a lot to learn about places and people.

CHAPTER 24

Homesick

"I also carried a flashlight, a long piece of rope and inflatable tubes."

By 1949 I hadn't been to Honolulu since a week after the war ended in 1945, and I was dreadfully homesick. The house on Beach Walk was still rented to Julie Hayes for her dress shop, and so when Mary and I went, we stayed with Mom and Dad at Mokuleia. Mary was fourteen months old. She had tottered all over the plane and poked her fingers into the food on the trays the stewardesses had collected. Finally, some kind woman volunteered to hold her for me, and I got a little rest. Jet planes were not in service yet and it was a nine-hour flight.

Mom, Dad, Mary, and I went to Mokuleia. The house had been restored since the 1946 tidal wave, but all summer we picked up pieces of broken glass left over from the destruction.

Mary was not supposed to get near the ocean about two hundred feet away, but that didn't stop her from trying. She wasn't able to walk down the slight incline to the water, and so she simply went down backward ooshing herself on her tummy. I discovered her before she got too far, but it was a pretty good example of how independent she would be the rest of her life. A chip off the old block.

Leslie Pietch and I had a luncheon at a club. It was just great to see everyone. Someone asked me if I was getting a divorce since my husband wasn't with me. I was shocked. I was learning about gossip and how some people thought.

By the time Jim actually did arrive in Honolulu for his two weeks vacation I was overjoyed to see him. We reunioned in the usual way and we began to discuss having another baby. Seemed like a great idea to me since we were still five away from my anticipated half dozen. Books such as *Cheaper by the Dozen* were coming out, and large families were in.

We had begun, with this trip to Hawaii that summer, a pattern that we were to follow for the remaining years of my parents' lives. Every other year we would be sent tickets for the plane trip from California to Hawaii. Our favorite plane was the Boeing Stratocruiser. It had a large cabin in the rear with two beds and a wash basin. We also flew on some Pan Am flights where we actually had berths and were able to sleep the trip away.

I used to dress Mary, Fran, and Stephanie in matching outfits. They looked pretty adorable. When Drew arrived, his shirt would also match. We would depart Fresno all dolled up, and by the time we got to L.A. an hour later, the outfits were a total mess after breakfast on the plane. Eventually I wised up and traveled with fresh outfits to put on just before we landed in Honolulu.

I also carried a flashlight, a long piece of rope, and inflatable tubes. This was in case the plane went down, so I could tie us all together in our tubes and could use the flashlight in case we got separated. This was ridiculous, of course, but it made me feel better. I remembered there had been a plane from Seattle to Honolulu that had gone down at night and some of the survivors said how much they wished they had had a flashlight, so I was prepared! I would breathe a huge sigh of relief when we would touch down at Honolulu airport. We'd made it one more time!

One long air flight the kids were entertained by an unusual person, a transvestite, a female impersonator. She\He was very tall, about 6'3," very exotic-looking and crazy about my kids. She gave them all a manicure and kept them happy, all the while applying the red nail polish. When we landed he said, "Be sure to come see my show at the Blue Angel."

Number 2 child, Frances Elizabeth, joined the family one very hot summer evening in 1950. She was born at Reedley , California Hospital. She was part of the new jet age, and her birth was fast and furious—jet-propelled. When Jim came to visit me after her birth, he was amazed to find me eating dinner with my lipstick still on.

Mother and Dad were with us again. They had visited us right after Mary was born in 1948 and that year we had rented two little cottages and Dad had spotted a lot overlooking the ocean in Pacific Grove, California, and had bought it for $1,500 and had given it to us.

In the Fifties, we borrowed money from Northwestern Life Insurance Company and hired a contractor and built a 1200-square-foot house on the lot, 829 Sea Palm in Pacific Grove, a short distance from Carmel.

My brother thought Mom and Dad had given us the house too. It was a misconception that caused all kinds of

Homesick

problems later on. We paid $63.98 a month for twenty years until the mortgage was fully paid off. It was going to be our retirement home!

I had a lot to learn about Jim Sorensen's retirement plans.

The summer Fran was born we went to Pacific Grove, again with Mary and with the new baby and with my folks. It was fine with us. We enjoyed the family togetherness. Jim's parents also came and stayed with Grandpa Sorensen, who lived in the big house next door to the little one we had rented.

This was the summer Mary swallowed a nickel. I called a doctor, and he said to feed her a can of baby prunes, which I did immediately. Later Dad took her with him when he went to the bank and when he got home he was laughing. Daddy laughed because he said Mary had made her first bank *'deposit'*!

We were fortunate some time after Fran was born to be given an opportunity by Alice and Harvey Chase to buy from them a piece of land about nine acres small or large, depending on how you look at these things. It was known to be too small to tractor and too large to shovel. Anyway, we were thrilled to be able to buy it, and we made plans to build a house on it.

We hired a bricklayer, found some hollow tile bricks in nearby Sanger, hired a carpenter, bought some huge beams to hold up the roof, consulted Harry Hunter in Fresno about the design, and began our next house.

It was totally different from the usual Orange Cove orange-growers dream house. It had a concrete slab floor, brick walls inside and out, and a composition-and-rock roof. The assessor for the county walked in the day he came to see how much to assess it for and he judged, "It looks just like a dairy barn."

Humph!

Well, it didn't to us! It was just very modern. We polished the floors with dark-brown wax, left the walls natural and with the high ceilings and the extra-large windows giving us a view of the mountains, we thought we had a rather elegant and different house. When the Tehachapi earthquake struck later that year, 1950, we grabbed Fran out of her crib and Mary out of her bed and ran outside. We were all safe, and the new brick house was sound and uncracked.

We had three outside patios—one in front that was walled in for privacy, one at the side with the jungle gym and the swings, and one at the back with the chaises and the outdoor dining table. Later we added a swimming pool and a tennis court and a baseball diamond. We were our own park and playground.

We experienced small-town hospitality the night we were given a very surprised house warming. We heard cars on the gravel driveway and went to the front door to investigate. We couldn't believe our eyes.

There were dozens of smiling people carrying casseroles, chairs, card tables and tablecloths and plates and glasses and silverware, and they simply moved in and took over and set up everything needed for a large dinner party. We were bowled over! And they were happy that we had not been tipped off.

I was experiencing real Hawaiian hospitality in Orange Cove, California.

CHAPTER 25

The Family Grows

"Listen, Bet, you don't pay attention to the church, you just love your husband."

We had four children born to us between 1950 and 1958 while we lived in Orange Cove. Dr. Robb Smith delivered them all. I loved the excitement of the delivery.

I loved being the center of attention, but the last one, Sally's birth, cured me of that. Dr. Smith and his nurse talked all through the delivery and the nurse sipped on a Coca-Cola and the two of them ignored me completely. I might have not been there. All my deliveries were easy and uncomplicated, and I am grateful that I never once had a miscarriage. I was 'old hat' to Dr. Smith.

Actually we moved to Visalia in April 1958, the year Sally was born. I was six months pregnant when we moved. We named her Sarah Louise *Napua (flower)*, the only one of our five to be given a Hawaiian name.

Stephanie Cutten, number three, was born four days before Christmas and so she was perfect to play the Christ child in our pageant. She weighed eight pounds and the doctor had predicted a boy. I can honestly say that when I saw her reddish hair and the curl in the middle of her forehead, I was in love. I had prayed for a docile baby and the dear Lord heard my prayer. She was totally calm and happy.

On the feast of the three wise men, January 6, 1954, we wrapped her in make-believe swaddling clothes, and laid her in the top bunk of the doll bed, and we dressed up like the Wise Men and paraded around the house singing "We Three Kings" and came to kneel and 'worship' at her side. She slept through the whole program.

Later on, when she was old enough to walk around outside, she loved to spy a slim, hard, cookie-shaped piece of dirt and bite into it! She also walked in the rain dragging her doll through the mud. Nothing disturbed her serenity. Her pet name was Mrs. McGoosey. The baby sitter in Hawaii called her a tame baby.

When we knew Drew, number four, was expected I wagered Dr. Smith *double or nothing*. A boy meant double payment (his usual fee was $100.00) and another girl meant no charge. The morning he was born all the nurses stayed after their shift to see what Mrs. Sorensen had *this* time. When Jim and I left for the hospital that morning in 1955, Mrs. Rogers, our devoted baby-sitter, was at home with the girls, and her last words to me were, "Don't bother to come home unless it's a boy!"

Well, you can imagine our amazement when the doctor looked at Drew's *ule* (guess!) and then went to announce, "Well, Jim, persistence pays!"

We tried hard not to show how elated we were and so it was probably a week before we let ourselves jump for joy! I remember hollering "Yippee!" and leaping up and down repeating and repeating, "Thank you, thank you, dear Lord."

The Family Grows

Well, about this time I was very aware of the Catholic Church's campaign for natural birth control otherwise known as the rhythm method. We were still young and ignorant too, and we tried natural birth control, and by the end of 1957 we were expecting number five.

Jim by this time had opened his own civil engineering office in the Bank of America Building about twenty miles away in Visalia. We had outgrown, or were soon to outgrow, our nice house in the country in Orange Cove.

I went house hunting in Visalia as soon as possible. Everything I saw was too small, too expensive, or did not have a big yard. Finally, I went to see Nancy Moock. Her husband Bob was a great friend of Jim's, and she was a very hospitable person, and I knew she wouldn't mind me dropping in on her. She listened to my story and then said, "I think the Kabo house is still for sale."

When she described it, I was amazed because I had been by it and had admired it from the street. It was a large gray wooden Victorian house with double columns flanking the front door. A porch ran around several sides, two large palm trees heralded the front, a large shade tree on the side and, best of all, a huge yard and only two blocks from the church and the school. An answer to my prayers. It was known as the Ben Maddox house. It reminded me of all the beautiful two-story houses on Nuuanu Street in Honolulu.

This was my first venture at house hunting, but I strode up the long front walk and clacked up the four wooden steps to the front porch and rang the bell next to the pink door. I could hear vacuuming going on.

Presently after I kept ringing, the vacuum stopped, and a beautiful older woman opened the door. It was Velda

Kabo. She wore her blond hair pulled back in a bun. Her large eyes were twinkling, and her low-pitched voice invited me in.

"Yes, we were thinking of selling the house. No, it is not on the market, and I will show you around and then your husband and my husband, Rodie, can talk. Oh, and by the way, the doorbell doesn't usually work."

I was utterly mad for this house. It had three bedrooms, two bathrooms, a living room, formal dining room and already-remodeled kitchen on the first floor. The old water-tank house had been converted into a fourth bedroom with washbasin and sleeping porch on the second floor. On the ground floor was a bathroom, a laundry room, another kitchen, and a bedroom. It was being rented out as a little apartment.

That night Jim and I got a baby-sitter, and we drove to Visalia and sat in the car and gazed longingly at the house and discussed the merits of building versus buying ready-made. Up and down we talked and talked and figured and figured.

I was going MAD with analysis.

I just knew I had to have that house. There was also the problem of paying the asking price of $24,000 and the problem of what to do with our house in Orange Cove.

As usual I announced that I would pray to St. Joseph. He had brought me a wonderful husband, and so he would find someone for our house in Orange Cove and would help us with Velda's house.

I prayed for a sign, and then we took the kids to Disneyland and talked all the way down, and on the way home we drove them by "the house," and they were

The Family Grows

thrilled with it too.

To make a six-weeks story shorter, we rented our Orange Cove house on a five-year lease, and the renters paid the first year in cash before they moved in. One problem solved.

Then Rodie Kabo called to say they were unsuccessful in finding a lot to build their duplex on, and if we would quit claim sixty feet off the back of the property, he would reduce the selling price to $21,000. Second problem solved!

ALL PRAYERS ANSWERED! That St. Joseph is quite a guy!

Jim was pleased with the new price and terms, and we opened an escrow. The day the escrow papers were ready for signatures, Jim was away on business, and I drove into Visalia and went to the title company and signed.

Little did I realize that fourteen years later, as a real estate broker, I would be be waltzing in and out of title companies on a regular basis.

On a lovely day in April, the movers loaded up the moving truck and tied on the swing set, the jungle gym, and the garbage cans, and we drove out the gravel driveway headed for our new life in Visalia. It was April 26, 1958.

Virginia Vortmann, godmother to Stephanie and Drew prophesied, "You'll be back in six months"

"That's what you think," I muttered under my breath. She drove to Visalia in the week that followed and helped me unpack boxes. I was six months pregnant, and I knew I was in Visalia for good.

Two weeks later, May 1958, my cousin Louise Johnston and two of my aunts, Nellie and Lottie, arrived for a one-week visit. Nellie, you recall, was a Seaton Sister of Charity.

Born and Raised in Waikiki

Jim was wonderful to them, but I was ready to have them leave after two days. Every night was a huge dinner in the dining room.

Aunt Nell was in seventh heaven with the church only two blocks away. She'd chug down there in her robes at least twice a day.

One night Nellie excused herself from the dinner table in order to use the bathroom. We could hear the tub filling and then utter silence for the next hour. She finally emerged in her night clothes.

We had all been wondering **"what the heck is she doing in there!"** I finally got a look-see because I had to give my own kids their baths and get them to bed. There on every rack was Aunt Nell's laundry. She had washed her bibs, her underwear, stockings, and her other apparel, and there was not one drop of water on the floor, and everything was utterly tidy.

The next year I had another letter from my aunts asking to visit again. I gathered my courage along with my wits, and I wrote them that it was out of the question with my current family responsibilities.

I was finally grown-up.

All this time we had a little cabin at Wilsonia Village in King's Canyon National Park, one hour's drive from Visalia. I had spent some time up there with the children, but I didn't like being up there without Jim. I used to get spooked at night and have nightmares. Also, the house only had an outhouse and had so many cracks in the floor and the walls that the varmints could get in. I could hear them gnawing the wood on the outside. Still it was fun, and we drove to the campground for a hot shower now

The Family Grows

and then and we drove to Hume Lake for a swim, and we also drove to the creeks in the area and bathed in them like the Indians. On July 29, 1958, when Sally, number five, was born, Mom and Dad were on hand to help out. My mother was ecstatic at the prospect of cooking a pork roast on the wood stove up at Wilsonia. It was going to be reliving her childhood on the farm in Willows, California.

My dad, the big-city guy, was apprehensive at staying in a house on beds that were not comfortable and the thought of using the outhouse appalled him. So once again we hired the carpenter to go up and build a small bathroom, and Dad also bought two Simmons twin beds.

The first night my Dad couldn't breath due to the altitude of 6500 feet and after three nights of no sleep, he begged off, and we drove him to Visalia and then I went back up.

A short time later we all gave up, and the folks went back to Waikiki. Before my dad went back to Waikiki I had a memorable conversation with him. We were driving down Lovers Lane in Visalia, and I brought up the subject of the Catholic Church's opposition to artificial birth control. His words were memorable to me, "Listen Bet, you don't pay any attention to the Church. You JUST LOVE YOUR HUSBAND!!"

End of sermon and the best advice I ever got.

I always loved my dad because he said it like it was, and anytime I asked him for advice he never ducked the real issue, and he respected the fact that I really needed an answer straight from the shoulder. My dad!

So the family did not grow anymore.

It was time to raise them.

Born and Raised in Waikiki

Before our son, Drew, was born our friends predicted that if I had a boy, he would be a big sissy since he had three older sisters. Well, hmmf! His third grade teacher called me in one day and told me I had to admonish Drew and make him settle down. He was disrupting the class. I said to her, "I am afraid he'll be a sissy, and I have not had any experience raising a boy."

"Sissy! Drew is the most masculine little boy I have ever known." After that conversation, if he misbehaved, we punished him. It was a relief to know we could.

I had fun with my kids. I made sure that living in our house was fun for them. And together, Jim and I taught all of them to work as well as to play.

I remember our dinners so well. Mostly I remember that at times I felt like the cook and the entertainer too. They came to the dinner table with clean faces, combed hair, washed hands, and healthy appetites.

Once I remember I said something like, "Why don't you all think of something to talk about and then I'll not talk. I'll just let _you_ talk."

DEATHLY SILENCE! No one said a word.

The idea of just sitting down and silently eating all the food on your plate without exchanging some pleasantries was outlandish to me. I needed conversation like a THIRSTY PERSON NEEDS WATER.

I used to plan surprises just to stir them up a little. I remember one time I served a hot rock right out of the oven. It looked like one of the baked potatoes that were on the other plates. The person who got it yelled, "Hey what is this?" and everyone exploded with laughter.

One day I read about the Surfer's Diet. It had lots of

The Family Grows

good ingredients, including Karma. So I went to the grocery store and bought all the ingredients but they didn't have Karma. So I went to the Health Food Store and asked the salesperson if she carried Karma. She laughed and asked me if I knew what Karma was? Of course, I didn't. She laughed again and said, "Oh, Mrs Sorensen, Karma is brotherly love!"

We had lots of that. We would steal a delicately appealing morsel off someone's plate after we had diverted their attention, "Hey, who swiped my steak?"

We cleared the table and did the dishes by playing a game. We drew from a deck of cards to see whose turn it was. High card clears.

Once I served them dog food in a fancy casserole. Drew had kidded me about the current TV ad for dog food that looked good enough to eat. I bought some canned dog food and baked it in a casserole and then set the casserole on the table for everyone to help themselves.

Drew lifted the lid, sniffed it, put his head down close to it and sniffed again and then exclaimed, "SAY, WHAT IS THIS STUFF!"

I think I laughed so hard I wet my pants.

Instead of answering five kids questions about what's for dinner? I would put the menu of the day on the refrigerator door.

For spending money I invented things to do: Washing inside windows (15 cents a pane), outside windows (25 cents), vacuuming the rooms (fifteen cents a room), ironing simple flat things (five cents each item). I always paid up the minute the job was done. If they delivered my bills, I paid them the face value of the stamps. They pulled lots of weeds too. And took out many shrubs and trimmed up many trees. Consequently they always had money to spend.

On the subject of spending money, I have to say that I always told the kids that no one gave Daddy money without him working for it and so I didn't think it was fair to give them money unless they worked for it. They seemed to understand.

No, they did not get an allowance until they got to high school.

As for raising children so that they turn out to be grown-ups, I am absolutely convinced that frustration, struggle and discouragement help a person to grow up. Believing this, it becomes a terribly urgent question of how to give these things to children for whom we desire only success.

Is it true, therefore, that a loving parent expresses greater love for her offspring when she in fact frustrates them occasionally?

She even watches them struggle at tasks too large that perhaps may lead to their discouragement, in the hope that in the end the good character and strong heart she knows is in them will triumph.

Does a loving parent always make life easier at all times and in all ways? I believe children in comfortable homes need to be challenged. They need to know how to cook and sew and how to run the washing machine, how to change a tire and how to work hard at whatever is necessary.

The worst message they can receive is that they are wealthy and will never have to work. I guess what I am saying is that I respect work for all, whether girls or boys.

The Family Grows

I suppose anyone who raised kids in the Sixties should mention what it was like. All I can say is Jim and I prayed a lot, and personally, I got along best with a non-confrontational stance. By 1966 and thereafter we had someone at U. C. Berkeley for the next dozen years.

Mary started it off. Her advisor at Redwood had attempted to persuade her not to go to Berkeley. Berkeley was experiencing the Free Speech Movement and lots of rebellion. It was pretty daunting to think of sending a young girl into that atmosphere. But I called her advisor and advised him to mind his own business, "Our family has gone to Berkeley for generations."

Lucky for Mary and for us we met a young girl who was going to Berkeley that year. I asked her how she liked going there to school and she replied with fervor, "I LOVE it. Where else can you go to school and hear Madame Nu and Malcolm X?"

That did it. So off to CAL went Mary. The day Governor Ronald Reagan called in the National Guard I called and asked her if she didn't think she'd better come home for a few days until everything calmed down. Her immediate answer was, "Oh, NO! I MIGHT MISS SOMETHING!"

Mary was followed to Berkeley by Fran and Stephanie and Drew. They all succeeded in getting good educations and in making us proud to be there when they graduated. Fran met her future husband, Stanley Taylor, III, at CAL. and through him and his family, Lois and Stan Taylor from Honolulu, Drew met his future wife, Leslie Long, also from Honolulu and niece of my old friend Leslie Long Pietsch. As someone said, "Betty Dyer is doing a good job marrying off her 'coast *haole* (Caucasian) kids.' Right on.

Our youngest, Sally, had decided when she had sex-education in second grade that she wanted to be a nurse. Believe it. When her time came to go to college, she still wanted to be a nurse, and so four years later she had her B.S. in nursing from the University of San Francisco.

Also in the Sixties, our president, John Kennedy, had vowed to have a man on the moon in this decade. The astronauts had flown around the moon at least twice and had made observations and we had all prayerfully watched the rockets blast off and held our breath when they returned to land. It was an incredible time in history.

We would lie outside at night and search the heavens and locate tiny pin-points of lights traversing the sky. The heavens were no longer just for the stars and the planets. We now had satellites on their endless travels through space enhancing our life on earth. We had better radio and television transmission worldwide because of the satellites.

Finally, in July of 1969 the MOON LANDING was scheduled. It seemed totally unreal, and at the same time totally feasible. When the big day came we were ready. We had the camera set to take pictures of the TV screen. We were all gathered in the family room in the house at 601 North Encina Street in Visalia, California.

Aunt Shirley, my husband's sister, and Uncle Chuck, her husband, drove down from Fresno to join all of us for this historic moment. The excitement was unbearable. The astronauts were speaking to Houston via satellites, and we could plainly hear them describing the appearance of the moon.

We could thrill with them as they made the final descent

The Family Grows

onto the moon's surface. We peered at the TV screen watching the space ship and praying for its safety. Finally we heard this, "The Eagle has landed."

"Aaah...!"

When the door to the space ship opened, and the ladder came out, we could plainly see the moon's surface: all barren, and no sky or mountains or trees or water. But it was the moon all right. Then we could see a bulky figure in a space suit slowly descending the ladder, and finally we heard a voice say, as he put his foot on the moon, "That's one small step for man, one giant leap for mankind."

We sighed with relief and with the glory of Neal Armstrong's words.

The second astronaut, Buzz Aldrin, came down the ladder next. The American flag was shoved into the surface of the moon by the two men. We stayed glued to the TV screen, afraid to leave for fear we'd miss something.

The third astronaut, Michael Collins, was keeping the spacecraft in readiness for the return trip back to our planet, Earth.

Finally, the moon walk was over, and the capsule buttoned up, and Michael Collins fired the rockets to propel the ship off the moon and back into the earth's orbit and the eventual safe return.

It was all real, yet unreal.

Also in the Sixties, the country suffered the pain of the assassinations of our President, John Kennedy, and of his brother, Robert Kennedy and of the Civil Rights leaders, Martin Luther King, Jr. and Malcolm X. It was a terrible decade of violence. We endured the agony and disappointment of the Vietnam War and were thankful our son,

Born and Raised in Waikiki

Drew, was too young to go.

We also lived through the Civil Rights struggle, and I began to look at black people with a new eye to equality. I watched the nightly news and saw the Freedom March from Selma to Mongomery, Alabama. I saw white adults screaming at little black children.

I read *Black Like Me*, and I reminded myself that our constitution grants equal rights. "All men are created equal." Although I had no desire to march with Martin Luther King, Jr., I was becoming aware of my changing feelings towards black men and women.

I would deliberately sit next to a black person on the bus. Instead of "them" and "us" it was beginning to be just "us." I saw the movie "Guess Who's Coming to Dinner" and, all in all, my attitude was intent on perceiving black people as individuals, some good and some bad, just as I observed white people.

So the turbulent Sixties came to an end, and our kids were coming of age, and we were all still friends.

CHAPTER 26

Brain Surgery

". . . and that is where Drew found me on the floor by the toilet."

I date my brain surgery by remembering when Mary Sorensen graduated from Redwood High School, I was there with my wig on. So proud and happy to be alive and to be there, and not causing grief to my family. So that would mean that the surgery was in 1965, April 2, to be exact.

I had been having terrific headaches for several months. I was cranky as all get-out too, and so I had consulted Dr. Smith and he had prescribed a mild tranquilizer. He thought raising five children had gotten me into this pathetic state. I would go to sleep with a headache and wake up with the same headache. It actually hurt more than ached.

On the day I fainted, I had driven to a party in Tulare. After I got home, I went into the bathroom and that is where Drew found me on the floor by the toilet. He was eleven years old.

Our family doctor made a house call and immediately ordered me into the hospital where a spinal tap was made and blood was found. This meant further tests had to be made, and Jim loaded me into the station wagon where I could lie down, and he checked me into St. Agnes Hospital in Fresno, forty miles away.

The first thing I noticed was a crucifix on the wall. It was comforting to know I was surrounded by people who shared my faith in God.

Immediately flowers began to arrive from our friends: the Nashes, Fergusons, Chandlers, Dofflemyers, Courtneys and cards by the dozen. I was amazed at the outpouring of encouragement. My favorite card said, "Don't worry you'll soon be on your feet. We just sold your car!"

I remember there was a beautiful young Apache Indian woman in a room nearby and one day I heard, "Psst, will you hand me my Ex-Lax. I won't scalp you!"

She was going in for back surgery and she knew she'd have trouble later on when she was recovering. I didn't hesitate. I handed her a laxative and wondered who would do the same for me later on.

I felt pretty happy about the attention, but definitely concerned about the outcome from all the tests. Finally, a week after I entered the hospital, Dr. David Zealer sat by my bed and explained, "There is something up there and we are going to take it out." I don't think he ever said the scary words "brain tumor." He was so gentle, and I had complete trust in his abilities.

The day of the surgery I was mentally ready. I had talked to Vi Ginsberg and told her I was not afraid, that I "had my faith," and I remember Violet saying "God bless your faith." No one had ever said that to me. I talked to my friend Peggy Laughlin, and she told me "everyone is praying for you."

Brain Surgery

So it was finally time.

They rolled me onto a gurney and wheeled me into the O.R. Jim walked along as far as they'd let him go. We reassured each other as best we could that everything was going to be alright.'

Jim's voice broke, and I held on to his strong hands and told him I was not afraid. We both had tears in our eyes.

Once in the O.R. I was dazzled by the blinding brightness of it all. Lights all over the place, and shiny objects reflecting the light. The nuns in the operating room welcomed me and smiled their angelic nuns' smiles. I felt completely at peace.

This was a big moment of truth and I was more than prepared for it all. They began to shave my head and when they were finished I asked for a mirror so I could see how funny-looking I was.

"Oh, Mrs. Sorensen," and they laughed with me when I saw my bald head.

That's all I remember about the O.R. When I woke up nine hours later in the recovery room I remember how cold I felt. Loving hands covered me with a cotton weave blanket. Then I couldn't seem to relax enough to sleep. The nurse finally gave me an injection and then she said, "You're going to like this but don't get used to it."

I floated in nirvana for several hours.

When I woke up Jim was there looking very relieved and happy to see me feeling so well, and I was terribly hungry. I complained that I needed something to eat, "after all I've been through." Jim later told me that was music to his ears.

Dr. Zealer came by,

"Well, it was benign and I think we got it all."

Instead of kissing his hand and expressing my utmost relief and appreciation, I said something flippant like "I guess it was easy" or something like that. He looked shocked and hurt.

I regretted saying it immediately and fortunately later I was able to express my deep appreciation for his genius. I discovered something, and that is that doctors are human and like to be thanked too. I wish I had a dollar for all the times I have said some flippant words when I should have thought before I spoke.

All the children at George McCann School prayed for me. Our youngest child, Sally, was in the first grade. She must have wondered how come her mother was the one they were saying prayers for. Stephanie and Drew were also at GMC. Fran by this time was in high school and Mary was waiting for "Pomp and Circumstance."

I've never asked them how they felt for the four weeks I was out of their lives. They must have done some soul searching of their own. Jim drove to Fresno every evening to sit by my bed and find out how I felt. When I got strong enough to walk, he held my hand and supported my side. By this time I was beginning to be my old self again. I remember one night I said, "Don't you have something better to do besides coming to see me!" Later Jim told me he felt good when I said that because he knew I was going to get completely well. My old blurting self again.

The euphoria lasted for several weeks.

You just can't imagine how it feels to go through something so life-threatening and to come out whole with a real future still in store. I exulted in my faith and in my health.

Brain Surgery

I couldn't thank the doctor and the nurses enough. And after three weeks post surgery, I was ready to go home and take up where I left off.

My recovery was complete.

Dr. Zealer had warned me that I should not smoke ever again, and so I never did. He also said I would probably not be able to smell with my left side of my nose. But that didn't happen. As far as I or anyone could see I was the same as ever.

Only I wasn't.

I took Dilantin for ten years and saw Dr. Zealer annually. From time to time I would get a slight headache, and sometime I would wonder if I was about to die. I would say a quick Act of Contrition and calm myself, and the feeling would pass. This went on for at least ten years. My head was my weak spot, and if I had stress, it would remind me to calm down and to calm myself. Finally these episodes passed and stopped altogether.

The kids grew up and went on to college and life became less stressful.

One more thing I want to tell you. After I came home from the hospital around the end of May, I asked Sister at school if I could take Popsicles to the entire school as a celebration of their prayers being answered. She agreed, and I took the treat, and that's when it occurred to me that I had been an instrument of God's Grace.

All two hundred and fifty precious children had prayed for me, and their prayers had been answered!

Amazing grace.

CHAPTER 27

Jim Sorensen

"He knew what he wanted and lucky for me he wanted me."

Now that we have been married forty-nine years this year of our Lord 1995, I can speak with authority on the subject of James Francis Sorensen.

Since this book is my story, the most important thing you have to remember about Jim Sorensen is that he loves Betty Dyer and has spent the last forty-nine years trying to please her. I don't deserve such devotion, but I'd kill anyone who tried to take it away from me.

Our time together has been and is a fast-forwarding blur of events. When I married Jim, I placed my hand in his and knew he would always take care of me. I had prayed to St. Joseph for a good husband, not necessarily Catholic, just a real man.

Jim's major good points are kindness, gentleness, courage, and self-determination. He always had his eye on the doughnut and not on the hole. He knew what he wanted, and lucky for me, he wanted me. He stands very straight at 6'5" and weighs around two hundred pounds. I think he is very handsome in a clean-cut way. He looks like a Navy man. He has great legs, and his eyes are green. Jim

Jim Sorensen

is a marvelous driver and he can repair almost anything. He is conservative in his outlook and is a linear thinker which drives me crazy sometimes.

He is cautious about money. He pays a bill the day it arrives. He can spend it if necessary, but he is not profligate or wanton. I don't think he ever has more than two hundred dollars in his wallet, and most of the time he's close to the end and has to get more. It just goes.

Jim is a modern man in many ways. Once I started to do real estate in 1972, he would insist on doing the dishes after dinner. He didn't fold diapers when the babies were little, but he did helpful things such as taking one or two of the children with him when he was making the rounds out in the country. He is undaunted by a dirty diaper and can still do the honors if one of his grandchildren needs attention.

One of my most tender memories of Jim is the night he sang our first grandchild to sleep. Frances Reath was then about three years old. She had gotten used to being sung to sleep every night. Jim and I were visiting her parents in New York City, and it came Jim's turn to sing her to sleep. I was curious to know what he would sing since he is not a singer. I sneaked into the nursery, and I heard Jim crooning the University of California Fight Song! And there was little Frances with her eyes closed, snoozing peacefully.

He feels that women deserve equal pay for equal work, and what's all the shouting about? He can't really understand why a woman would want to go to war but he does understand that that is the way it is. So he doesn't waste his breath and energy flailing against women.

His four daughters have probably educated him more

than we realize.

Sometimes I catch him wondering if we can afford to live if he does not earn. It's as if he is worried the money will run out. Well, in my opinion, that is just an excuse to keep on working. Like many professional men, his work friends are his real friends since he doesn't play golf or socialize with just men. He has spent his civil engineering career protecting the water rights of the San Joaquin Valley farmers and in trying to get the Congress and the state legislators to agree to develop more water resources. It has been an uphill battle and very discouraging at times.

He has made a difference.

He has been President of the National Water Resources Association and has served on the Governor's Task Force in California well as the Engineering Advisory Council of the University of California. For many years, he has served on the Legislative Committee, the Executive Committee and the Board of Directors of the Associated California Water Agencies. For over thirty years, he was the Executive Secretary and Engineer for the Friant Water Users of the San Joaquin Valley of California. He has been very busy.

The plain truth of the matter is this: Jim Sorensen likes to work, and he likes his work.

If I were to list the things he likes work would be at the top of the list. He also likes ice cream. In fact he craves ice cream. Duck hunting would probably be a close second to work.

Jim also likes his children, his car, his boat, his house, his wife. These are not listed in order of importance. I don't think he separates them.

Jim Sorensen

He also likes music, and he likes to read. His hobbies would be sailing, traveling, and reading. Now these are all good things. But I'll just mention a few faults, so whoever reads this will not think I'm married to a saint.

For instance, just suppose you are riding in the car with Jim and you want to go a little faster. Your eyes notice that the speedometer is on thirty-five miles per hour and you feel like you are on the back of a tortoise. So you gently and quietly say, "Do you think we could go a little faster?"

Whamo! He pushes the accelerator to the floor, and now we are rocketing along at a terrifying speed.

He hates any suggestion that he is not perfect, and he reacts 180 degrees. So I guess you can say Jim Sorensen has a healthy male ego. Yet, he is not conceited. He is almost too modest at times.

He seldom lets me finish a thought without taking the opposite tack. Maybe this is what it's like after forty-nine years.

I say to him, "Why can't you be like one of my girl friends and gossip with me without taking the other person's side?"

I have had to assert my conversational rights. Equal time to speak is what I am talking about.

He is much more conservative than I, and so I think of myself as a closet liberal. He is a politician, and I hate politics. Despite these differences we get along very well, most of the time!

It is the little things that irk. I can say it is probably going to rain, and he will say that there will not be rain for at least the next five days.

I remember telephone numbers, and he can't remember

a number for thirty seconds. He says remembering numbers just isn't important to him.

On the plus side, he is a great joke teller. I love to hear him tell a story. He tells them well and everyone else enjoys them too. Ask him to tell you the one about the blind man who got on a bus.

I'll always love him, because he understands me. He has given me a lot of room to grow and lots of support. I have never felt tied down. Whenever I needed to get a taste of Waikiki we'd go there, or he would understand that I had to go by myself.

One time we were in San Francisco and I mentioned that I'd like to go visit my Mother for a week.

"Why don't you?" he encouraged, and a few hours later I arrived back in Waikiki with my toothbrush and my nightie in a paper bag.

Well, speaking of my mother makes me think that she was crazy about Jim. His Jimmy Stewart style of dry humor appealed to her, and she positively drooled over him. It was a kick, and of course it pleased Jim no end to know what a hit he'd made.

The above one-week trip in the early Sixties included a drive out to Mokuleia to visit the old house on Crozier Drive. By this time Mother was living in Waikiki in a condominium with her nurse, Margaret Simpson, and was nearing her eighties.

On this day, I drove Mom by herself out to the old house she had built in 1933. There was no place she would rather have visited. And I liked to drive out there too.

We got to the house and opened it up. I settled Mom on the chaise on the ocean side *lanai* (patio) where she could feel the breeze and see the coconut trees she had planted. She sighed with pleasure. She could smile, but with the Parkinson's disease, she couldn't really carry on a conversation. Just one look at her face and her eyes were all I needed to know how happy she felt.

Her tile-top table was still there—the scene of so many hard-fought Bridge battles with Clara and Hugo. Pop's double bed was in the corner surrounded by windows and the painted screen still there for privacy.

The *punee* (couch) Mom had made and Dad had kidded her about was inviting me to stretch out by the large windows facing the ocean. I decided to sweep out the house first. No one had been there for months. When I swept under Daddy's big double bed, I was horrified to sweep out dozens of dead centipedes about three inches long. Very dead and dried out. I couldn't believe my eyes. I remembered how Pop had always sprayed a lot of FLIT all around his bed before he retired for the night. So the residue of bug spray had worked even years later.

Another time I asked Jim if I could go to Honolulu by myself for a week. This time I had a definite plan in mind. I was going to buy a place at Mokuleia Beach Colony on the North Shore of Oahu. I didn't discuss it ahead of time with Jim. I was just going to do it and I didn't want anyone to try to talk me out of it. I had some shares of Castle and Cooke to use for the down payment. I had received it from my Mother upon her death in 1968.

I arrived at Honolulu airport on a United Airlines flight. Jack had left his daughter Katy's little Volkswagen in the parking lot at the airport. I was to have the use of it for the week. It was ten o'clock at night. I headed out to the country thirty miles north, and when I got to the house at Mokuleia it was so dark by the front door, that I had great difficulty seeing where to put the key. Luckily for me, the next door neighbors heard me and came to investigate with a flashlight and helped me to get the key to work. What a relief!

I was all alone in the house I so dearly loved. The memories flooded over me.

I opened the fridge and found it empty except for a single beer. (Thank you, Lord.) Then I telephoned Jim to say I was safely in the house and all was well.

Then I took off my clothes and left them on the floor. This was my first taste of a new kind of freedom with no one telling me what to do. I'd be messy if I felt like it.

Then I chose the bed I would feel most at home in, threw back its covers to make sure there were not any bad bugs waiting to nip my toes, and checked all the doors for locks and finally went to sleep. It felt mighty strange to be all alone for the first time in a very long time. I slept well.

After a good breakfast I called Sandy Parker Real Estate to inquire about sales at Mokuleia Beach Colony, a five year old condominium project down the beach from where our old house was. Sandy lived at the Colony. He told me that two units were on the market. One was 15B on the ocean for $36,000, and the other was 5A on the golf course for $31,500. I had been advised not to buy on the ocean because the salt air ruined all the appliances. It was more or less a moot point, because the price was more than I could handle anyway. 5A had the original 5% mortgage with about $21,000 left to pay off. That was the good part. The bad part was the color inside. All the walls had been painted a bright papaya orange.

I wanted to offer $29,000 since I was just getting into being a realtor and I heard one could make an offer. Sandy said the price was firm, and if I wanted it I'd have to pay the asking price. Knowing I had the Castle and Cooke stock to sell for the down payment to the loan, I said, "O.K. Sandy, we'll go."

I had heard my Dad use that expression, and I felt very hip and savvy saying that. I was elated!

Now all I had to do in the remaining days of my one week was to paint the place off-white and to buy a queen-size bed and headboard and a rug and a few other improvements. I worked frantically, but I was so happy to have our own place.

I applied gallons of off-white paint, drank numerous beers, and sang along with Myrtle K. Hilo singing "Drinking Champagne, Feeling No Pain."

Francis Fujioka, Waialua's famous grocer, very kindly guaranteed my check at the furniture store in Waipahu where I bought the bed, etc.

"Sure, anything for you," he said.

I still had a few days to go. At night I worked on a quilt, and by week's end it was finished. I also lay on the beach and peered at the view and decided to paint a picture. My energy was enormous.

I called my old friend Babbie and she invited me to come see her mother. Mrs. Henshaw was still living in the gorgeous Hawaiian-style house on the stream by Oahu Country Club. We called her Aunt Rosie. She was as glamorous to me as ever. It was something about her speaking voice. She wore a muumuu with long sleeves and a high neck. As

I recall, it was a pale pink print. We sat on her *lanai* and "talked story" and laughed at our remembrances and ate the Dobash cake I had brought from Wahiawa.

The breeze from the Pali rustled the ginger, and the ferns and I pinched myself to think of all I was doing in this one week of my life.

When I returned home at the end of the week, I told Jim about buying the place at Mokuleia and he said, "I knew you were up to something."

I told you that guy understands me!

Here's a play that depicts our typical conversation.

"Do You Know Where Your Children Are"

(a comedy in one act)

Cast: Jim as played by Jim and Betty as played by Betty.

As the curtains open, we see a distinguished, tall, tweedy man seated in a comfy chair at stage right. In the background can be heard a female voice humming "Tiny Bubbles" and an occasional audible sigh.

Jim: Say, have you talked to the kids this week?

Betty: Are you talking to me?

Jim Sorensen

Jim: Who the heck do you think I'm talking to?

Betty: You don't have to shout and the answer is NO.

Jim: Answer to what?

Betty: Answer to your question, bug brain. NO I HAVE NOT TALKED TO or spoken with any of the kids this week.

Jim: Thanks.

Betty: You're welcome. Dinner's ready.

Betty appears from behind the curtain with a tray full of dinner stuff. She is wearing an apron which she takes off and flings on a chair after she sets the dinner things on the table.

Jim: Are we ready? (He says this brightly.)

Betty: No, I'm just practicing setting the table.

Jim: To get back to my original question if you haven't spoken with anyone this week, why don't we call them after dinner.

Betty: Why not! We'll try Mary and Henry first. They are in California for two days. Then we can call Bermuda and see how Dick and Stephanie are.

Born and Raised in Waikiki

Jim: After that we can call Honolulu and get the report from Sally and her boyfriend.

Betty: Yup, and next week we can call New York and have a word with Fran and Three. Do you suppose if we call Drew and Les they'll be home?

Jim: Possibly but I doubt it. Aren't they going to Cayucos for a wedding and reunion?

Betty: I gotta go to the mall after dinner and get something.

Jim: What? I'll go with you.

Betty: O.K. I'm gonna get a bumper sticker that says "DO YOU KNOW WHERE YOUR CHILDREN ARE?" I never needed one before.

Curtain

CHAPTER 28

Haina Ia Mai Kapuana
(This Is The End of My Story)

"A little girl from Waikiki singing on Fifth Avenue."

So this is the end of the story about the girl who was born and raised in Waikiki.

Sometimes I feel I take things too seriously. Which is why I went to the library one day and asked the librarian to recommend a book on humor. She asked,"Do you want a book of jokes?"

"No, not really. It's just that my husband and I are getting too serious, and I want a book that will explain how to have a sense of humor."

"Oh, Mrs Sorensen, I think that's funny."

I give up. There really isn't a book that does that. The ability to laugh at things comes from within. So I am working on it.

I haven't mentioned my Real Estate career.

It lasted seventeen years, and I made a lot of friends and quite a bit of money and was darn glad to get out of it. Many of the times the telephone rang, it meant there was a problem somewhere. I met quite a number of termites and found out that sellers can lie just as much as buyers.

For example, one time I listed a house for sale and another agent sold it. When we had the structural report done, it was discovered that the second shower did not drain, not at all. When I spoke to the seller about this she told me that it had not been working for YEARS, and she hadn't bothered to tell me ahead of time. Oh, brother!

I never got sued, but I got locked inside a property one time. It happened like this.

My partner Jane Nash and I had sold a beautiful Southern Mansion-type house in the finest neighborhood for the highest price that had been paid for a house in Visalia up to that date, something around $400,000.

We were one week from closing the escrow. Another realtor had tried to go around us and ruin our deal and sell it to someone else while it was in escrow, and so we were anxious to wind up all the parts of the transaction and get it over with.

The last hurdle was the final inspections of the electrical, plumbing, appliances and swimming pool, etc.

We had made appointments with all the necessary experts, and in addition, I had made a date for lunch.

At around 9:30 in the morning I met the first of the inspectors at the property. When he had completed his job, I awaited the next inspector. This one sat by the curb and bleated on his horn.

I went out to the gated entrance, and that is when I discovered that the first inspector had locked the gate behind him, and I didn't have a clue how to operate the security gate. It was shut! Period. I was locked in. He couldn't get in and I couldn't get out.

I attempted to leave by crossing the creek next to the property and going around the fence but a large police

Haina Ia Mai Kapuana

guard dog stopped me. Nice doggie.

I telephoned various lock people but no one could give me the combination for this particular gate.

I canceled my lunch date.

The owners had moved to Los Angeles the week before, and my last resort was to locate them. It was not easy, because they were being sued for bankruptcy, but the escrow person in Beverly Hills finally gave me the number when I explained my predicament.

So I telephoned and this is what the wife said to me,

"BETTY, WHAT ON EARTH ARE YOU DOING IN MY HOUSE?"

I nearly died. After four frustrating hours this question!

I let her have it! "MRS M. I AM TRYING TO GET ALL THE INSPECTIONS DONE SO THAT YOUR ESCROW CAN CLOSE AND I AM LOCKED IN YOUR GODDAMN PROPERTY AND HOW THE HELL DO I GET THE GATE TO OPEN?"

She gave me the combination.

Haina hou.

I can't end my story without just a few words about my first love—singing. More than a Real Estate lady, I am a singer. I LOVE to sing.

I have had some great times onstage, alone like the first solo at Punahou as well as with friends at the conventions and on cruise ships.

We had a group that entertained with Hawaiian music at water conventions—Bob Chuck, Charlie Parker, Brother Hohu, (all from Honolulu), Ted Riggins, (from Arizona) and me. We sang our repertoire, and judging from the applause, it was enjoyed.

Born and Raised in Waikiki

We opened our show with "Little Grass Shack," added "Pearly Shells," "To You Sweetheart Aloha," and other favorites. My special number was "The Pidgin-English Hula." Our debut was on the stage at the Biltmore Hotel in Los Angeles. We were a hit and it grew into a very happy combination.

I remember one special time in San Antonio, Texas, on the River Walk when Bob Chuck and I sang "The Hawaiian Wedding Song" from the stage of the amphitheater on the river. The setting was perfect, and there was a full moon, and we gave it all the schmaltz we had.

We still get compliments on that evening.

We have sung with congressmen and senators. It is surprising how many prominent people like to sing, and how many can play an instrument. We'd gather in the presidential suite at the hotel where we were all staying, and we'd sing for hours.

When the National Reclamation Association met in Honolulu a few years ago, I had the thrill of singing on the stage of the Hilton Hawaiian Village—over a thousand conventioneers were there, and we sang for them. I made up new words to "There's No Place Like Hawaii" and later on I led them all in the closing song of "God Bless America." I felt like Kate Smith.

When we cruised for two weeks on the Greek ship in 1989, I tried out for the Farewell Show and made the cut. I sang "To You Sweetheart, Aloha" and "E Maliu Mai." The audience spoke many languages. I dedicated the last song to Irmgard Farden Aluli, the composer. I sang it in Hawaiian, and they loved it and understood it.

So I have my own corn patch. Put a mike in my hand

Haina Ia Mai Kapuana

and let me loose.

Currently, I am singing with the Sweet Adelines. They are an organization of women who like to sing barbershop harmony. There are several thousand of us all over the world. I sing the Bass part. The other three parts are Tenor, Lead, and Baritone. We put on makeup and false eyelashes and once a year we compete with other choruses and wear flashy costumes. It's Show Biz. The more sequins the better.

In 1993, Jim and I were in New York City for Christmas and I sang in front of the Plaza Hotel with the Salvation Army bell ringers. They put a mike in my hands and I gave it all I had with "O Holy Night." A little girl from Waikiki singing on Fifth Avenue.

I don't know if I am still waiting for some man to do what he has to do but I don't really care. I am happy.

Vivre, c'est choisir
et chaque jour recommencer:
C'est au coeur d'indiquer
la route.

To live is to choose
and each day begin again.
It is the heart which indicates the way.

The Kaddish

"Let the glory of God be extolled. Let His Great Name be hallowed in the world whose creation He willed. May His kingdom soon prevail in our own lives and the life of all Israel and let us say: Amen.

Let His Great Name be blessed for ever and ever.

Let the Name of the Holy One, blessed is He, be glorified, exalted, and honored, though He is beyond all the praises, songs, and adorations that we can utter, and let us say: Amen.

For us and for all Israel, may the blessings of peace and the promise of life come true, and let us say: Amen.

May He who causes peace to reign in the high heavens, let peace descend on us, on all Israel and all the world, and let us say: Amen."

Chronology

October 20, 1915 John Michael Dyer and Mabel Corrine De Jarlais married at St. Augustine Chapel in Waikiki, Hawaii

August 10, 1916 John Francis (Jack) Dyer born in Honolulu

February 4, 1922 Laura Elizabeth (Betty) Dyer born in Honolulu

November 1925 Visit Parker Ranch on Big Island

September 1927 Enter first grade at Punahou School

June 1929 *SS Wilhemina* to Portland, First trip to mainland

June 1931 *SS Empress of Japan*. Second trip to the mainland

July 1933 *SS Empress of Japan*. Ohio and Chicago and Los Angeles with father.

July 1937 *SS Empress of Japan* to Yokohama, Japan

August 1937 War breaks out in Shanghai, China

August 1937 Bombed by the Chinese on the *SS President Hoover*

June 1939 Graduation from Punahou School

July 1939 *SS Mariposa* to Australia. *SS Orontes* from Sydney, Australia to Naples, Italy

Sept 1939 England declares war on Germany after Germany invades Poland

Sept 1939 *SS Empress of Britain* from England to Quebec, Canada

Sept 1939 First visit to New York City

Sept 1939 Freshman year at Mount Holyoke College, South Hadley, Massachusetts

June 1940 *SS Monterey* to Honolulu for summer vacation

Sept 1940 Return to Mt. Holyoke College for sophomore year

June 1941 Transfer as a junior to Stanford University, California

Sept 1941 Return to Honolulu on *SS Matsonia*

Dec 7, 1941 Japan attacks United States at Pearl Harbor and Hickham Field and Wheeler Field, Hawaii

Dec 8, 1941 United States Congress declares war on Japan

Reath, Jr.

Mar. 19, 1978 Frances Olivia Reath born in NYC

Aug. 28,1978 James Shattuck Taylor born in Lafayette, CA

Mar. 26,1981 Graham Clawson Taylor born in Lafayette

Aug. 6, 1982 Drew Severin Sorensen marries Leslie Kahailiopua Long

Sept 18,1982 Stephanie Cutten Sorensen marries J. Richard Fredericks

Jan. 22, 1985 Matthew Foley Fredericks born in San Francisco

Dec. 4, 1985 Kurt Austin Sorensen born in Los Angeles

July 25, 1986 Colleen Sorensen Fredericks born San Francisco

Oct. 10, 1986 Alannah Laura Taylor born in Lafayette

Feb. 7, 1987 Sally Sorensen marries Timothy Edmond Howard

Oct. 1, 1987 Tyler James Sorensen born in Visalia

Feb. 14, 1988 Peter Albrecht Howard born in San Francisco

Aug. 7, 1989 Michael Dyer Howard born in Menlo Park

Sept 13, 1990 Will Norman Fredericks born in San Francisco

Mar. 1, 1991 Kathryn Victoria Howard born in Atherton, CA